BOOKS

John Michael Chambers' book *Trump and the Resurrection of America* is an indispensable aid for understanding the significance of Donald Trump's presidency. Mr. Chambers not only deals with the significance of Donald Trump as a person, he deals with the historic significance of the voters who elected him, as well as the elemental concerns that drove them to do so.

Mr. Chambers understands that the United States is in the midst of a critical battle for the survival of the American identity. He understands that the challenge to that identity is part of a crisis of Western civilization, a crisis that reflects the efforts of a global elitist faction to overturn the constitutional self-government of the American people.

The voters who invested their trust in Donald Trump have made him the focus of the battle to thwart this faction's aim. Mr. Chambers deals with several key aspects of this battle, and is especially informative when he discusses those that involve the economic and political challenges the United States must overcome if the constitution and liberty of their people is to survive. He even deals with the implications of the stranglehold that the ruthless profiteers who dominate the pharmaceutical sector now have on both the bureaucratic and legislative aspects of America's institutions of law and self-government.

Like Donald Trump, Mr. Chambers is clearly aware of the primordial importance of preserving the moral basis of the Constitution and positive identity of the American people. We should pray that he soon deals in an equally comprehensive way with this existentially most important dimension of the vital challenge President Trump's Presidency must face and overcome.

For every person who is sincerely interested in understanding the critical nature of America's current crisis, *Trump and the Resurrection of America* is required reading. This is especially true, however, of voters who know that the future of their country is staked upon the fulfillment of his Presidency's positive promise for America.

> ~ *Dr. Alan Keyes,*
> *Former Presidential Candidate*
> *US Ambassador appointed by Ronald Reagan*
> *IAMtv.US*

"I received a PDF copy from the author, with whom I share many concerns about and hopes for the Trump Presidency, and am truly delighted with all that he has done. As a former spy who also co-created the Marine Corps Intelligence Activity, and went on to found the Open Source Intelligence discipline, I deal every day with complex nuanced topics that I find very difficult to explain to normal people. This author has done a BRILLIANT job, a PATRIOTIC job, a LIFE-ENHANCING and GOD-BLESSED job, of laying out both the threats to the Trump Presidency and to America, and the threats and possibilities for resurrecting America and saving it from the Deep State I know so well.

The chapter on Agenda 2030, the UN's nominally well-intentioned, but actually deeply threatening hegemonic goals, is worth the price of the book alone, and I have asked the author's permission to extract and publish that chapter. Nothing is what it seems if you are a normally educated person who relies on the mainstream media (Crap News Network, New York Compost, and Washington Poop) for their information. This book is education and valuable - politically, culturally, economically, and ethically - in every possible sense of the word. BRAVO!

~ Robert David Steele, Former CIA, Nominated for Nobel Peace Prize 2017

"I couldn't agree more with the book's premise: Our very survival as a sovereign nation is at stake. The outcome of the next four years under Donald Trump will determine if this is a new beginning, or America's Last Stand. Do not underestimate this man's capabilities: President Trump will smoke out the career politicians entrenched in D.C., and aggressively take on the unelected, self-appointed globalists who crafted Agenda 2030 and the Sustainability Goals. He will confront, and demand, change from Big Pharma, Big Oil, Big Agra, Big Banks and the Far Left Environmentalists. If you're short on time, read Chapter Seven, a brilliant analysis of Agenda 2030, and Chapter 19, with detailed tables comparing Trump's ideas for freedom vs. the enslavement goals of the New World Order. We can make America Great Again, faster than ever, but we must be active participants. This book shows us how."

~ Dr. Sherri Tenpenny, Physician, Author, Speaker. Middleburg Heights,
OH. www.Vaxxter.com

"John Michael Chambers has written an outstanding book that will stand as the benchmark of scholarly, historical works on our Constitutional Republic. It covers past, present and future America, and is relayed through an extremely good grasp of our history. It shows how perilously close to collapse our nation came, fiscally, morally and politically, and how that happened. It also portrays how we are not out of the woods yet and gives us good, wise solutions to future problems that will occur. Americans have awoken, but not fully, to the perils of the World Shadow Government and their evil plans for us and the redistribution of American assets. We need to stand vigilant. America will remain that beacon of light to the rest of the world. This book is a must-read for every America-loving patriot, regardless of party affiliation."

~ Fred Brownbill, Patriot and Retired Deputy Sheriff, Florida

John, I knew you would be busy when you left for your trip in 2011. Thank you for writing this book. You made this insane world make sense by showing history and connecting the dots. We can see what the lack of history has done to divide America. This should be required reading in all schools.

> ~ *Karen Schoen, Florida American Freedom Watch Radio, Radio Host on blogtalkradio.com/americanstatesman*

Every chapter is full of insightful information, and provides an in-depth perspective from Chapter One - "The Election That Was Never Meant To Be" to the very last chapter, "By The Grace of God". Your book points out that "Making America Great Again" will not happen quickly, and every day we recognize that statement as true. Best wishes in all your efforts to continue the battle, and please know we support your efforts.

> ~ *Marina Woolcock, President Republican, Federated Women of the Villages*

SPEECHES

John Michael Chambers gave a riveting speech to a large group of patriots from the St Lucie County Tea Party. During his discussion, you could hear a pin drop, as the entire audience sat on the edge of their seats, clinging to his every word. As a truth seeker, John encouraged everyone to pursue their own truth, rather than conforming to a pre-determined construct or ideology. Equally important, he inspired everyone to bravely pull back the layers of the matrix, while simultaneously capitalizing on individual strength, as well as the strength of the like-minded collective. Clearly, John Michael Chambers has a message to share that no American-loving patriot is going to want to miss. If you have not heard him speak, I profoundly recommend you seize this opportunity to schedule this highly esteemed, thought-provoking author at your next event. I can assure you; his speech will rock your world. WWG1WGA!

> ~ *Kelly Lynn Ruiz, St Lucie County, Donald J. Trump for President Chairman*

John was extremely well-versed on the subject of the "Deep State". He provided an excellent and insightful discussion of how our nation and Constitution has been used, abused and taken for granted by these forces for years. I believe he is correct in his analysis of Mr. Trump's strategy for turning the tables on these forces and taking the nation back. I also believe that John's sense that God has definitely put Mr. Trump in place for this time is spot on. I would highly recommend this talk for anyone who loves and cares for America. This is needed information and we must not only learn it, but begin to face, head on and aggressively, the evil of the Deep State. I look forward to hearing more from John!

> ~ *Glynnda White, Event Director, Winter Haven 912*

John Michael Chambers spoke at our recent meeting of the Polo Republican Club in Boca Raton, which included many politically-savvy activists. We were all impressed with his grasp of current and future issues. He provided information that was a revelation to this knowledgeable group. Few know the workings of the political realm in this country better than John. He would be an excellent speaker for any group.

> ~ *Dr. Howard D. Zipper, President, Polo Republican Club of Boca Raton*

Women For Trump Sarasota Manatee enjoyed hearing from John Michael Chambers at our May 6 meeting. Mr. Chambers was interesting and engaging. He offered information about topics, such as Q, that many of our members have never heard about. We were very happy to have John Michael Chambers join us!

> ~ *Caroline Wetherington, Founder, Women for Trump*

John, thank you very much for being our keynote speaker. You put it all on the line, letting truths be known, good or bad, be as it may. It was rewarding to hear you speak of "The Matrix" - FOX News in the manner that it deserved. The members and guests were enthralled by your truths and could not get enough of your librettos. Many express that you were the best speaker we've ever had. The way that your books evaporated was astonishing. John, you are truly masterful in your presentation. The topics and related information (truths) were brilliant. One member misplaced her notes (I think that they were probably picked up by someone in error) and spent a good 40 minutes looking for them, amazing!

> ~ *Mary Waller, Chairwoman, Federated Republican Women's Club of Naples*

POLITICAL ACTIVISM

"I have known John Chambers since our early days together at the Save America Foundation. John is one of the most relentless, tireless and ruthlessly honest people that I have ever known. He is funny, engaging, street-smart and knows how to think outside the box. He is a dedicated patriot and a visionary. His gifts are numerous, but he remains a humble man of dedicated purpose. Best of all, John knows how to get things done. He doesn't just sit back and complain, or take pot shots at people who are fighting the good fight. He pitches in and helps where he can. I am honored to have known John, and count him as a dear friend."

> ~ *Richard Davis, MD, Florida*

"I have known John for about ten years, both professionally and personally. We have jointly written a book together, worked on numerous other projects, and spoke around the country at conferences and on radio shows promoting financial, economic, and religious freedom. John has the tenacity of a bulldog with a "larger than life" heart to help people.

> ~ *Kirk Elliott, PhD, ThD, Colorado*

"John is a man who cares very deeply about people and who is always looking to help and offer opportunities to anyone looking. He is an "out of the box" thinker and a person who will look at situations from a unique perspective. I am honored to consider him my friend, and always look forward to every time we can get together."

~ *Alex Snitker, Former US Senate Candidate, Florida*

"I have known John for several years. He is kind, gentle and honest and his integrity is beyond question. He opened my eyes to the dangerous path that we are on, and we did what we could to warn the people around us of that danger. Listen to this man and follow his advice!"

~ *Kevin Quinn, Computer Programmer, Florida*

"For many years I have followed the adventures of John Michael Chambers as he circled the globe, and I've traveled with him across the USA. I've admired his creativity, drive and ethics while working with him in the recording studio, the radio station and on stage. From all these experiences, I have formed a deep bond and admiration for John. I fully endorse anything he takes on as he is one of the finest men I've ever known."

~ *J Todd Plant, Entertainer, Vocalist/Musician, Florida*

To Tom,

TRUMP AND THE RESURRECTION OF AMERICA

Leading America's Second Revolution

JOHN MICHAEL CHAMBERS

DEFIANCE PRESS
& PUBLISHING

Trump and the Resurrection of America: Leading America's Second Revolution

ISBN-13: 978-1-948035-33-0 (Hard Cover)
ISBN-13: 978-1-948035-34-7(eBook)

Published by Defiance Press and Publishing, LLC

Bulk orders of this book may be obtained by contacting Defiance Press and Publishing, LLC at: www.defiancepress.com.

Public Relations Dept. – Defiance Press & Publishing, LLC
281-581-9300
pr@defiancepress.com

Defiance Press & Publishing, LLC
281-581-9300
info@defiancepress.com

"First they ignore you, then they laugh at you, then they challenge you, then you win."

Mahatma Gandhi

"I am asking you to believe in yourself again, and I am asking you to believe in America. And if we do that, then all together we will make America strong again, we will make America wealthy again, we will make America safe again, and we will make America great again. God bless you!"

Donald J. Trump

Together, we will save America...

TABLE OF CONTENTS

SPECIAL THANKS

A very special thanks and credit to contributing authors Dr. Sherri Tenpenny, DO and Dr. Richard Davis, MD., Kirk Elliott, PhD, ThD

SECTION I: BEFORE WE BEGIN
Laying the groundwork

ABOUT THE AUTHOR

JOHN MICHAEL CHAMBERS IS A REGISTERED Republican, presently residing in Tampa, Florida. John is an author, speaker, and national media commentator. He is also the Chairman of the Sarasota Patriots for Trump group. John was the founder of the Save America Foundation, a 501(c) (4) not for profit. In Washington, D.C., John attended meetings held by members of Congress that were also attended by former President, George W. Bush, and First Lady, Laura Bush. He was awarded by the Presidential Business Advisory Council of Washington DC, 2004 & 2005, The Businessman of the Year Award for the state of Colorado.

John is a patriot who loves his country and serves as but one voice for humanity. John organized group meetings, roundtables and large-scale conventions across the country. John has been interviewed in the Wall Street Journal, CBS, NBC and many on-line media platforms, including talk radio throughout the country. John has dedicated much of his time and resources, often times at great sacrifice over the past two decades, sharing insightful and empowering information to help keep freedom alive. John is an avid supporter of President Trump.

Author

John is a prolific transformational author challenging even the most awakened reader. He has authored seven books to date. His latest book, "Trump and the Resurrection of America", was nominated for the 24th Annual Colorado Independent Publishers Association EVVY Awards. John has also written nearly 400 articles to date that can be found on his website. His next book will be published in March 2020, and is sure to be very well received.

Speaker

John has spoken publicly to date in dozens of cities, eight states and three countries, where he addresses the impact of globalization and the changes and challenges facing not only Americans, but all of humanity. His speech covers the most critical political and economic issues of the day as President Trump takes on the Deep State. John is a most sought after speaker in the state of Florida. He is upsetting apple carts everywhere he goes with his "no-holds barred" speech on the Deep State, the cost of illegal immigration, voter fraud and current topics that patriots are talking about. The "JMC weekly Report" is a paid subscription keeping patriots informed, empowered and connected. John continues his book signing, public speaking tour, all across America.

News Commentator

John is a sought after political commentator covering all the important issues of the day like no other. Television, radio, YouTube, and internet-based platforms reach out to John on a weekly basis to get his views of the events as they are unfolding. America's second revolution is underway. John engages and captivates audiences, addressing current, trending, political, economic and Deep State issues of our time.

Wealth Strategist

John Michael Chambers retired in 2008 as a successful financial advisor, with a total of six independent offices in three states. John is not a financial or investment advisor today, nor does he manage money for a fee. John serves as a "Wealth Strategist" and coach, providing independent non-biased commentary and analysis. John's proprietary model is truly a paradigm shift in thinking, offering a new sound, superior, proactive approach to protecting and preserving wealth, utilizing both alternative paper assets, as well as tangible assets.

While so many others will continue to operate in the deceitful and flawed modalities being advised by an industry they no longer trust, John's clients are positioned properly for the **Global Financial Reset** that is upon us. A great change is now underway. The time for action is now. When working with John, you gain access to John's valuable Rolodex, a highly respected resource network of like-minded economists and financial professionals who can become part of your team.

An Open Letter from Me to You

Hi there, and thank you very much for spending this time with me right here, right now. It is by no accident that we met. I believe by first reading this open letter, you may have greater insights into not only me, but also into the subject matter that I have taken on here within the pages of this book. I believe, due to my journey and experiences that I am somewhat in a unique position to write this book at this precise moment in history.

I just wanted to fill you in as I summarize from a broad stroke approach the path I have traveled on this journey called life. I don't want to bore you with the details from 1958–1995, so I will begin this open letter by starting out from 1996 up until the present time. I believe that if I share the experiences I had between 1996–2008, this will set the stage for the material you are about to read. Thank you. It's an important read. Let's begin.

Heeding the Call

In 1996, I embarked upon a career as a financial advisor by procuring first my insurance license, then my securities licenses, later followed by industry awards, acclimations, certifications, and designations. This career as an independent financial advisor began in the state of Florida, and, by the time I retired in 2008, I had six offices in three states: Colorado, New Mexico, and Florida. I also held licenses in almost a dozen states in total. Please do read on.

Being a self-made nobody from the school of hard knocks, a graduate of the University of Life and Living, a self-employed entrepreneur of sorts, this leg of my journey was a tremendous learning experience. After all, I had met with so many people from all across the country who were mostly retired, had successful careers, were professionals, or owned a business, and all were senior to me in age, as my focus was on wealth preservation via estate and retirement planning. Many of my clients were in their fifties to eighties. I was in my forties. Yes, these clients (and their families) learned and benefited from the products and services that my firm and I provided, but I, too, learned from *them* and the life experiences they shared with me. I am still connected with some of these clients even today, twenty years plus later.

I was a member of the prestigious Million Dollar Roundtable. MDRT, the Premier Association of Financial Professionals® founded in 1927, is a global, independent association of more than 49,500 of the world's leading life insurance and financial services professionals from more than five hundred companies in over seventy countries. MDRT members demonstrate exceptional professional knowledge, strict ethical conduct, and outstanding client service. MDRT membership is recognized internationally as the standard of excellence in the life insurance and financial services business. I had achieved what only one-half of 1% of over 350,000 insurance and financial advisors worldwide have achieved, and that is a seat at the "Top of Table." Yes, I had reached a marked degree of success, and had the opportunity to meet and learn from so many professionals from all walks of life via the international associations I was a member of. So, why did I resign from this career at forty-nine if all was going so well?

Well, you see, the more I learned, the more I knew, and the more I grew. I had reached a point where I needed to heed a higher calling. Unwinding a successful going concern at the top of my game was not an easy decision, nor an easy task, but nonetheless duty calls and I transitioned my business and stepped onto the next road of my journey. But what did I see? What is it that I had learned? And what was this higher calling?

Yes, we took advantage of current tax codes, trust planning, and designed creative plans to create wealth, structured tax advantaged income planning, and leveraged estates for future generations. But it was money that we worked with. I worked with money, investments, insurance, annuities, mutual funds, IRAs, trusts, etc., and this put me right in the lion's playpen along with lawyers, Wall Street, and the insurance and banking industries. They, of course, were all playing in the playpen with the government. I think you now know where I am heading with this. But I must first digress. I guess you could call me a "recovering financial advisor." ☺

Disruptive, Uncomfortable Truths

Twenty-two years ago in 1997, just as I embarked upon this path of being a financial advisor, a friend gave me two things to review. One was a two-set VHS called "The Money Masters"[1] and the other was a newsletter called "The McAlvany Intelligence Advisor."[2]

This changed everything. It is of course by no accident this data was placed in my hands and at that precise moment. It's a funny thing what happens to people when they are presented with *disruptive, uncomfortable truths*. It can trigger an instant denial with unwarranted attempts to discredit what they have seen or heard. It can also invoke "Okay, I get it, but there is nothing I can do about it anyway." Then they go on about the business of their day-to-day lives as though they had never seen nor heard the information at all. Then there is another response: "Oh my gosh, I knew something was not quite right. I had better look further into this." This was my response.

Having just opened my first office and being so excited about this new career as a financial advisor, I continued on that path for twelve

1 The Money Masters, https://www.youtube.com/watch?v=lbarjpJhSLw
2 https://mcalvanyintelligenceadvisor.com/

years and I am glad that I did. However, I needed to know more, as those videos and that newsletter served as a catalyst on my quest for more information, more concealed truths for me to uncover. So again, the more I saw, the more I needed to know. And so I embarked upon this path as a sort of parallel existence to my day-to-day life. This resulted in me being slowly transformed into a truth-seeking, critical thinker, and there was no turning back.

Then, on September 11, 2001, *everything* changed. It was time to speed up this quest for truth.

JFK – November 22, 1963, Dallas, Texas

I was five years of age. Not long after this tragic event, Americans began to question their government and rightly so. Even to this day, critical records surrounding the assassination of President Kennedy remain sealed. And more recently, with the tragic events of September 11, 2001, yet another American tragedy with scores of unanswered questions completely left out of the 911 commission report. But back to the Money Masters video set and the McAlvany Intelligence Advisor. What did I see? What had I learned?

I had always questioned things even as a child. I always felt I knew something was not quite right – to me, people and life made very little sense, but I could not put my finger on it. That all changed and was validated in 1997.

My research began in 1997, and bit by bit I was connecting the dots as things were not as they seemed. I mean, I learned that the Federal Reserve (who seized control over our currency in 1913), for example, was a private for-profit bank and is in fact unconstitutional. I discovered that our money system was really a debt-based system with no tangible backing that was creating inflation over time.

I began to learn why the U.S. was in a continual state of war and who was funding these wars and what the true objectives were. Each door that I opened led to more and more doors. This rabbit hole seems to be endless. It is so important to ask questions and then do your homework. It takes a fairly high degree of confront the deeper you get into all this, but, at the same time, your ability to have and experience these things increases.

The key, as I have learned over time, is to not become so negatively impacted but, instead, to become active. First a truth seeker, then a truth revealer. I'm sharing what I have learned with others and by becoming a part of the solution through a variety of proactive measures rather than caving myself in from the disruptive and evil things one comes to learn about. Cause and effect at play. I have also discovered that surrounding yourself with like-minded people who understand the times in which we live, and who have embarked upon the discovery of these truths, is also most beneficial. Much better than going it alone. I mean, after all, this is a dual-terminal universe, right?

Parallel Life

So, between 1997–2008, and certainly after September 11, 2001, I ramped up my sidelined studies in what I would now call the "parallel life" I was living. I was super busy working, developing, and growing my business, while all along my life was being transformed from what I was learning via my research.

At some point, you simply get it. *You just get it*. You see it. It runs as a pattern. Just as in the movie starring Jim Carrey, a must-see film called *The Truman Show*. They run the same sorts of patterns over and over again as in problem-reaction-solution, which I will go over later on in this book.

Media

My discovery about television and the media happened when I was about fourteen years of age, but, by this time between 1997–2008, it was evident that the media and Hollywood, etc. were a controlled delivery system of false data and disinformation controlling the thoughts of people, creating a false narrative and shoving their agenda down our throats; thus, creating a population of non-thinking, regurgitating robots – the robotic hypnotic flock. And now, thanks in no small part to Donald Trump, many others are beginning to see this too. I am not alone. It's refreshing actually and very positive as the pendulum swings both ways and the scales are now finally beginning to tip.

I left behind a growing, successful business that I had built from the ground up because the discovery of these *disruptive, uncomfortable truths* was just that – disruptive.

I could no longer play in the playpen with such poor bedfellows like lawyers, Wall Street, and the insurance and banking industries as I began to see the level of ethics and the corruption that was taking place. I also was NOT a fan of the repealing of the longstanding Glass-Steagall Act[3] that President Bill Clinton revoked.

It was also evident that the government was in bed with the big corporations, the Fed, and the central banks, etc. We all know how that works. I knew that markets were manipulated and controlled at the people's expense. I knew that the real estate and debt debacle was at our doorstep just prior to the 2008 collapse and had warned so many of this well in advance.

I knew about the questionable loans that were being handed out like candy to an unsuspecting child (thanks in part to Alan Greenspan and later Ben Bernanke, "Helicopter Ben"). I knew that all booms and busts are scientifically engineered and that the only ones that have long-lasting profits are in fact the banks and crooked corporations and governments. It was clear to me that the U.S. dollar was in peril regardless of its apparent strength (even to this day and even more so to this day).

We all discovered very quickly after Enron, then Lehman Brothers,

---

3 The Glass-Steagall Act, http://www.investopedia.com/articles/03/071603.asp

Bear Stearns, and Merrill Lynch, that the ratings agencies were also up to their eyeballs with the same dirt from playing in the same playpen with the corporations, banks, and government. We learned that FDIC was basically broke and does not even come close to protecting the amounts on deposit. Then there was the NSA, Patriot Act, Obamacare, Geo-Engineering, Common Core, Agenda 21, Agenda 2030, vaccines, FEMA camps, Dodd-Frank, HAARP, scores of executive orders, and many other bills that were deconstructing this once great nation bit by bit, day by day, over a period of a few decades. And, as of recently, we have transgenders, with penis in hand, urinating next to young girls in the ladies' room. We went from Kennedy putting a man on the moon to Obama putting a man in the ladies' room. Yikes! And please don't get me started with the PC (political correctness) BS. I can go on and on but I won't.

Turning Point

I decided that I could no longer do this. I could no longer be a part of the system's problems. I could no longer provide investment products and advice knowing all along that there was information about these products and about the overall system at large that could be detrimental to the client. And believe it or not, there was much that I was not permitted to disclose. The regulatory bodies that governed me due to the licenses I held pretty much controlled what I could and could not say or present to a client or prospect.

And so, shocking as it was to many around me in my life at that time, I retired from the financial services industry and transitioned my business and obligations over the course of about one year, not fun. In heeding my higher calling, what was I to do now? Where was this higher calling going to lead me? I surrendered my licenses (all in good standing) and transitioned my business. How was I to earn a living? What was I to do with this newly acquired knowledge? Where was I heading?

This brings us to a new fork in the road. The path less chosen, I might add. It took me a year or so to figure out how I could serve others and capitalize on my gifts, talents, and abilities. After all, I was now fifty years old, and having been self-employed much of my working life, I was pretty much unemployable in this new jobless marketplace in 2008–2009. So what did I do?

API

I formed the Asset Preservation Institute (API), a consulting company empowering individuals in a changing America. I assembled a team of experts I had developed relationships with over the years and arranged for them to be available to my clients. I provided roundtable group discussions and skyped in various experts like a PhD in public policy and administration, a PhD in economics, constitutional attorneys, trusted expert financial professionals, a precious metals firm, internationalization experts, and so many others from a broad spectrum of different fields.

Through private one-on-one consultations, I began to share my knowledge of the financial products and markets as they *truly* were. I provided independent analysis of what was really going on with my new client's portfolios and relationships, and believe me, this was eye-opening for my clients and proved to be most beneficial. In essence, I showed them how the game was played and what the true pros and cons and cost of their investments were and how the relationships worked, how people were paid, and so many other aspects unbeknownst to them at the time, including the corruption at the banking, Wall Street, and Federal Reserve level.

We began having conversations about alternative tangible investment opportunities like land development, private placement opportunities, and real estate both here and abroad. We began discussing gold and silver, how to buy it, how and where to store it domestically and internationally. We discussed paper to tangible ratios. We began talking about liquidity, inflation, and currency protection and becoming debt-free. It was not uncommon for us to talk about GOOTS (getting out of the system) as much as possible yet still growing, preserving, and protecting wealth.

We talked about having a Plan B in place due to the times in which we live here at home or living and investing abroad. The subject matter was always personal in nature and endless in scope. The result typically was a well-informed, well-connected client who was confident with their decisions and was in a better and more confident financial position and in control of their lives. Now, that is a good position to be in, wouldn't you say?

And since our financial wellbeing is probably the second or third most important aspect of our lives, with health, faith, and family perhaps being first, we began having discussions that followed this natural progression. Financial problems lead to economic problems. Economic problems lead to political problems. Political problems lead to geo-political problems, which typically result in currency wars, trade wars, and war-wars. We are deep into the latter part of this cycle as I write.

Freedom – It's Up to US

While running API (Asset Preservation Institute), I launched my own radio show on 860 WGUL in Tampa Bay, Florida. The name of my program was "Freedom, It's Up to US." The word soon began to spread about me, my network, and the services I was providing through API. It was around that time, as you may recall, when Rick Santelli from CNBC, on the bond trading floor of the Chicago Exchange, went on a rant on live TV against President Obama's tax plans and suggested we, the people, revolt like the Boston Tea Party did back in the day. And so we did.

Shortly thereafter it was Glenn Beck who then launched the 912 groups, and lo and behold Tea Parties and related groups of all kinds sprang up across this nation. It is important to note that in my opinion this "freedom movement" actually began a few years prior to this with "Campaign for Liberty" spawned by former Congressman Ron Paul's supporters. Truth be told it also happened in the 1960s, but they were crushed by the establishment (more on that perhaps in another book). "You say you want a revolution?"

I had the opportunity to meet with Ron Paul two consecutive years in a private board room meeting discussing ideas and strategies to get America back on track, along with suggestions for his campaign. The same people who are relentlessly assaulting Trump are the same people who ripped into Ron Paul and helped to prevent his election. I will talk about these chaps a bit further on in this book. And so the journey continued.

Road Less Traveled

Someone heard me on my radio program and showed up in my office. Long story short, this gentleman invited me to speak before a local Tea Party group in Florida. There were fifty to seventy-five people gathered in the back room of a Perkins restaurant.

The leader of this group was talking about the various issues of the day that many Americans were unhappy with at the time. He then called on me to stand up and speak, allowing me about ten minutes if that. Unscripted as I was, I immediately unleashed some hard-hitting sound bites about the true state of the economy and then launched into a condensed story of the Federal Reserve. Let's just say, to quote Renée Zellweger from the movie *Jerry McGuire*, "I had them at hello."

The room was somewhat shell-shocked, and the engaging questions began to bombard me. When I sat down at my table with a small group of people, I became surrounded by so many people asking how to get in contact with me. This leads us to the Save America Foundation.

I went back to my office that night and did a search and found that almost overnight there were all kinds of Tea Party and Tea Party related politically active groups sprouting up all over the country. County by county, state by state, I saw an engaged and highly motivated populace and thought, *"Well, this is a good thing. Perhaps we can turn this thing around and save America."*

After attending a few different local group meetings in my county, I decided to form the Save America Foundation, a 501(c) (4) not-for-profit corporation. Its mission statement was simple and clear, "To see that our elected officials reinstate, protect, defend and adhere to the U.S. Constitution, the Declaration of Independence and the Bill of Rights." The attorney who drafted my corporate articles, structure, and tax ID filing suggested I leave off the "reinstate" part as not to "piss off the IRS" so that we would be assured not-for-profit tax ID status. So I followed his advice, but once I got that tax ID number, I reinstated the word "reinstate" into our mission statement. To this day, eleven years later, we still need to "reinstate," and now, in one man's opinion, with President Trump there is true hope to do just that, as he has stated he will cancel all unconstitutional executive orders. More on that later.

Save America Foundation

From 2009–2015, the SAF (Save America Foundation) cut its teeth on the road to restoring America. These were very challenging times, as you may recall, right off the heels of the 2008 orchestrated market and real estate collapse and the un-vetted "selection" of Barack Hussein Obama (a complete fraud and the worst President in the history of this country in my opinion). So we had our work cut out for us. And for any Democrats, libertarians, or "other," I am no fan of George W. Bush, his father, and his granddaddy Prescott.

Quickly, the SAF gathered members first locally, statewide, and then nationally. We even had traffic on our website from well over a dozen foreign countries. After all, all eyes were on America, and the SAF, like Star Trek, went "where no man has gone before." We covered the uncomfortable, disruptive truths and taboo subjects that many groups steered clear from. Many embraced us, many rejected us. Time has proven us to be right.

We held live monthly roundtable public forums which were well attended. These forums were then posted on the SAF site to be shared with the world. We brought in local speakers, state speakers, and national speakers. We focused on several initiatives and built a diverse group of board of director members. We had dozens of committee and initiative volunteers as well.

So, one day I had this idea to hold a convention like no other to unite all the politically active related groups and reach more and more people to sound the alarms, as freedom was rapidly slipping away. The board and the SAF volunteers worked tirelessly to put on what to this day may very well be the biggest convention of its kind.

This event took place at the Marriott Hotel in Tampa, Florida, in 2011 and received national media coverage. It is noteworthy that, during the entire time of the SAF from inception to dissolution, not one BOD member or volunteer ever received one penny of compensation.

In fact, many donated not only their time and various resources but, in some cases, even their hard-earned dollars. I, for one, invested well over $50,000 into this foundation. I want to thank each and every one who helped this foundation, with a special thank you to the longest presiding president and founding member, deputy sheriff, and my friend until this day, Mr. Fred Brownbill.[4]

---

4 https://www.facebook.com/fred.brownbill

Save America Convention

The convention's headline speaker was Fox News contributor and legal analyst Judge Andrew Napolitano. I arranged for the judge to headline our convention, and introduced him at the opening night to kick off the event. I had the pleasure of meeting with him and speaking with the judge after he spoke. This was a well-attended three-day convention with many Tea Party leaders having traveled from afar in attendance. The speakers from this three-day convention are listed below; forgive me if I left anyone off the list as it's been many years now.

» Andrew Napolitano (Judge, Legal Analyst Fox News)
» Richard Mack (Sheriff)
» G. Edward Griffin (Author, Producer)
» Tom Tancredo (Former Congressman)
» Joseph Farah (World Net Daily)
» Stewart Rhodes (Constitutional Attorney, Founder Oath Keepers)
» Gary Johnson (Former Governor)
» Col. Mike McCalister (Ret. Military Candidate for U.S. Senate)
» Mark Adams (Attorney)
» Dr. Richard Davis (Founder PollMole, Activist)
» Dr. David McKalip (Neurosurgeon, Activist)
» Fred Brownbill (Deputy Sheriff, President, Save America Foundation)
» John Michael Chambers (Author, Founder of the Save America Foundation)
» Kirk Elliott, PhD (Precious Metals Expert, Author, Producer)
» Paul St. John (Vietnam Vet, Patriot)
» Mad Max Mullen (MSG)
» Frantz Kebreau (Black Historian)
» Alex Snitker (Former Candidate for U.S. Senate)

- » Mark Cross (Campaign for Liberty)
- » James Mell (Businessman, Corporate Consultant)
- » Keith Flaugh (Get Out of Our House)
- » Robert C. Brown III (Retired Marine, One Nation Under God)
- » Brandon Smith (Alt-Market)
- » Bill Bunkley (Radio Talk Show Host)
- » Karen Schoen (Agenda 21)
- » John Galt (Blogger)

The SAF went on to hold another two conventions – one in Grand Junction, Colorado, and one in the Denver area, and included private banking pioneer and author, Marilyn Barnewall, as well as many other speakers. These conventions received television, radio, newsprint, and online coverage.

Realist

I am a long-term optimist, but a short-term realist. By the late winter of 2011, I had come to the realization that America could not be saved by the individual and collective efforts of what I saw before me. I had been all across the country, worked with many Tea Party related groups and individuals inside and outside of politics. I had spoken before dozens and dozens of groups, held large-scale conventions, and I was becoming a good student of history. So, again, I had come to the conclusion that America could not be saved.

Those who know me well recall me saying back then that there is an awakening slowly taking place within the human spirit, and that the most unlikely people from many walks of life and from all over the world will begin to rise to the occasion. The world will have true leadership to rally behind and to support, and then we may have a chance to turn things around. Think back to 2011. This leadership was nowhere to be found.

This awakening was beginning to occur back then, but at an awfully slow pace. We are now well into 2019, and time has proven me to be right as the U.S. (and the world for that matter) continued from 2011–2016 to crumble under the false song of globalism. And so, just as those around me were very surprised when I walked away from my financial services career back in 2008, so were those around me surprised when I stepped down from the Save America Foundation, my radio program, and the Asset Preservation Institute, preparing to leave the U.S. altogether. Sorry, I am one who not only embraces change, but creates change.

Throughout much of 2011, I was in wind-down transition mode (at least in my mind), and by April 2011, I began the necessary steps for my departure. I spent the last nine months of 2011 wrapping up a thirty-city six-state public speaking tour. I handled the necessary steps preparing the foundation and institute for my departure.

API was transitioned to my associate Kirk Elliott, PhD,[5] who helped me to grow that business model. The foundation was in the good hands and leadership of the longstanding presiding president, Fred Brownbill, and the board of directors. I canceled my radio show. And so late December 2011, after a quick trip to New York to see family and friends, I flew to Asia for yet another road on this journey. Except this time, I flew over eight thousand miles away.

Abroad

I spent the better part of the next five years living in and traveling through many countries. People would ask me back home, "John, why did you leave the country?" My reply – "I did not leave my country; my country left me."

At the time, I had likened this to sort of a withdrawal wind-down phase. I was off the main hotspot battlefield (America) and kind of taking a breather and a backseat from a far, distant perch. It felt like

5 https://sovereignadvisors.net/pages/our-founder

I was sitting on the moon with my legs dangling, just watching the world go 'round and 'round, but, in actuality, I was in China. Yep, China of all places. This international journey began in China. I want to indicate that although I did in fact leave the battlefield if you will, I never left being available for people and I provided intel and resources via skype, phone, and e-mail. I maintained critical relationships.

From 2011–2016, I had been in China, Hong Kong, Tibet, Philippines, Thailand, Laos, Myanmar, and Belize, with perhaps only 10% of those years spent in the U.S. on a couple of sporadic trips. What was I doing, you may ask?

Well, truth be told, there was not a day that passed where my thoughts were not consumed with the rapid deterioration of America and the world. I was well aware of the sound of the ticking of the clock. This I could not escape, as it resonated throughout my cellular structure and in my feeling world. It is impossible to simply turn away or turn it off but, after having dedicated my life and sacrificed so much fighting the good fight for so many years, I needed to regroup. With whom? With me, myself, and I. Time to reassess. What had I learned? What had I accomplished over these years? Where was I presently, and what areas of my life needed "repair"?

What was I to do moving forward? All of this can be answered, along with all the experiences and adventures I had traveling and living overseas, in an entirely different body of work, as it goes *far beyond* the scope and purpose of this book, *Trump and the Resurrection of America*. I will conclude by saying that it has been among the best experiences of my life, and perhaps I will write about that in another body of work at another time down the line.

Paradigm Shift of Consciousness

Those who know me well from back in the early days of the Save America Foundation, I had stated that the most unlikely people will begin to emerge from around the world in the hour of need as part of this great awakening that I believe is taking place on a personal and spiritual level. You can see this on a one-on-one basis with people in your life. You can see this as well in some leaders and people in position of power and influence. You can easily see this on social media. Perhaps you can see this or feel this within yourself. Well, on June 16, 2015, we saw one of the most unlikely people to emerge on the global stage. One who would come to be the leader of the free world in what is arguably the most powerful position in the world. That person is Donald J. Trump. That position is President of the United States.

What One Man Can Do

I was living in Thailand watching Donald Trump blast on the scene, and it did not take me long to realize that this was for real. Not only was it for real, but it was a validation and assurance, at least for me, that my premonition and intuition had come to be. And so I was immediately inspired to write about the Trump Phenomenon. I launched my blogsite, John MichaelChambers.com,[6] and began blogging on a regular basis, with close to 400 blog posts now to date.

I had just finished my 2015 book, *Misconceptions and Course Corrections,*[7] and launched right into my next book, *What One Man Can Do – No Trump No Hope,*[8] which was published in April of 2016. All while living in beautiful Thailand.

For the first time in over five years, I felt there was true hope and a brief opportunity to save America and to turn civilization back onto a much-needed course correction. At the same time, my good friend Dr. Richard Davis, (R.I.P.), from back in the Save America Foundation days had been in contact with me, and we were discussing

---

6 https://johnmichaelchambers.com/
7 *Misconceptions and Course Corrections*, https://johnmichaelchambers.com/books/misconceptions-and-course-corrections/
8 *What One Man Can Do – No Trump No Hope*, https://johnmichaelchambers.com/books/what-one-man-can-do/

the emergence of Donald Trump onto the scene. We each had (and I still do) great concerns about the dangers that would lie ahead for Trump and America. One such danger was stealing the election from Donald Trump to name but one.

Dr. Davis, who has over four hundred patents under his belt and two companies that he took to an IPO with a combined market cap of a billion dollars, had been busy with yet another groundbreaking, revolutionary invention – a robust technological platform and app called PollMole. PollMole Technology Release 1.0 can detect and deter election fraud via the electronic affidavit, historical and unprecedented.

Beginning in August 2016 while I was still in Thailand, I provided assistance where and when I could in helping Dr. Davis launch his company. This led to Dr. Davis meeting with many people, including Steve Bannon, Joseph Farah, Roger Stone, Reince Priebus, Mike Pence, and Donald Trump himself just prior to the election of 2016.

Take Me Home Country Roads

The stage was set. Mr. Trump was the grounding force, the magnet if you will, which prompted me to return home. It was time to get back into the ring as this was America's last stand. As the Trump phenomenon accelerated, so did the shadow government and its henchmen mouthpieces and front groups' attacks on the Donald. I arrived in Florida in the last few days of September 2016, met with Dr. Davis and some other key figures in this freedom movement, as well as visited with family and friends, then off to Ohio I went.

Like so many others, I spent almost all my time doing all I could to help Donald Trump get elected. I did this from Thailand and then back here in the States. October and November were pretty much sleepless nights working practically around the clock. Then, on November 8, 2016, into the wee hours of the morning, everything changed. Donald J. Trump became the President Elect, historical.

Trump Wins – Three Times!

And so, Donald Trump goes on a "Thank You" tour to once again record-breaking crowds with thousands standing outside in frigid temperatures just to hear the Donald. Meanwhile, the delusional lunatics were in denial, shell-shocked that Clinton the criminal was not elected. And since Donald Trump was not supposed to happen, the stunned liberal left and the media mouthpieces continued to attack and assault Donald Trump. Since this was an election and not the standard selection rigged process, they tried to deny Trump of his rightfully earned election by first doing the recounts (which worked against them), then influencing the Electoral College (which also remained well in Trump's favor). So Hillary Clinton lost all three times, with Donald Trump (and freedom-loving people from all over the world) the victor.

What Lies Ahead

"Making America Great Again" will not happen quickly, nor easily. Some of the benefits may be realized somewhat early on, but most of the results of Trump's agenda (providing he is able to accomplish this) may take five, ten, twenty years or more to become fully realized. These efforts are more for posterity and will not come without challenges. We can expect President Trump to be infiltrated and given deliberate faulty intelligence.

We know for certain the media and the Deep State and Shadow Government will continue to chip away at Trump. If we thought this was a wild ride during the primaries and the general election, we haven't seen anything yet! Trust me on this. They, too, will double down.

And so, by the grace of God, and the power of the people, Donald J. Trump becomes our leader. The leader of the free world. This represents the most powerful driving force to not only resurrect America, but to set humanity on a much-needed course correction as President Trump leads America's second revolution.

Donald Trump represents true hope for so many in America and around the world, but the battle has just begun, and this will be a seriously dangerous phase that we are entering. How grateful I am that we have Trump in office, and so it is time for us to unite. We must unite with one heart and one mind.

In Closing

From September 2016 through January 2018, I had been in a series of meetings with some individuals regarding the situation of the nation, the election of Donald Trump, and what we can do to help strengthen this nation in its hour of need. I also spent time writing this book. My public speaking tour, based upon the content of this book, began in Ohio on February 4, 2017, has expanded all across America.

Truth be told, I am not really an "expert" in anything, but rather a "student" of everything, but I have done my homework and continue to do so. I continue to align myself with honest, competent people of like mind.

I am not afraid to communicate my thoughts, my feelings, my commentary and analysis, whether in the form of daily conversation, blogging, authoring books, writing, doing media interviews, public speaking, or consulting. And so therefore, I shall spend the majority of my time in the U.S. in 2019 and beyond doing just that. I intend to divide my time between the U.S. and Asia beginning in 2020 and beyond.

Time + Trump = a much more informed, engaged and united electorate. It's an exciting time to be alive, and it is my belief that we have this chance to perhaps turn things around for America and for the world. "We must not surrender to the false song of globalism." And so the battle begins.

INTRODUCTION

DONALD J. TRUMP HAS BEEN ELECTED President of the United States, so everything will be just fine now. He will simply "Make America Great Again"? And this is cause for celebration? Well, yes and no. I mean, happy days are here again, right? No, wrong.

With Trump's election, we entered 2017 with a sense of true hope and optimism, I, for one, as a long-term optimist but a *short-term realist*, can assure you of one thing: This may very well be America's last stand. There are no guarantees, and so much is at stake. These are the questions that need to be asked. Is Donald Trump safe from harm? Will Donald Trump actually be able to implement his agenda to Make America Great Again? Will President Donald Trump protect, defend, and adhere to the U.S. Constitution? Will he be the President of "law and order" as promised on the campaign trail? Will he be "his own man" and not beholden to the New World Order, Wall Street, the bankers or the Fed? It surely seems so. I will tell you this, since his announcement to run in June of 2015 (or shortly thereafter), he has had my full support and does to this day.

Introduction

Sushi, Navajo, Thailand, and Ohio

While drafting the final chapters of this book, before I sent it off to the publisher, something hit me. Something had dawned on me. I thought I had better get this into the introduction of the book. And so I did.

I walked into the local sushi bar and was waiting to be seated when a man started up a conversation at the cash register with me while he was picking up his "to go" order. I was wearing my Colorado coat made by the Navajo Indians. He complimented the coat (which strangers often do) and asked if I was a Native American. I said no, I was from New York and living in Thailand. He said, "Wow! Thailand?" He then asked what I was doing in Ohio on this cold winter's night, and I said that I was having some sake and sushi. "Oh, and I just wrote a book." He said, "Wow! A book? On what subject, may I ask?" I told him it was a book about the changes and challenges facing America and the world. He said, "Wow! What is the title?" I said, *Trump and the Resurrection of America.*" I waited. And I waited. I waited to read his response, both his facial expression and what he would say. And then he smiled (sort of) and said, "Wow! I will look out for that book and pick up a copy."

My overall read was that he probably was not a Trump supporter. I could just get that because those who are always express their support and unity once they find another Trump supporter. He did not. But he was unlike some of the people I will be describing here in just a moment. He had views that perhaps differed from mine, but realized we are all in this together, and he, too, wishes for a safer and more prosperous America as should we all. And if you don't wish for a safer, more prosperous America, then "get the hell out" as Trump might say.

So, in conclusion, the man expressed his interest in buying and reading the book to get all views as he, too, was concerned about the road ahead for America. He was a nice white man; I would say perhaps a family man in his early forties at best. He wished me luck

41

and took his sushi home. I am sure I became the subject matter at his dinner table. ☺

I was then seated at the bar. Since I do spend quite a bit of time alone, I started thinking I needed to add something to the introduction of this book. And so, just this morning, with a fresh pot of black coffee, I have added these next few paragraphs with the hope that…

A) They may resonate with the many Trump supporters and perhaps will be insightful when you confront the non-Trump supporters in your life.

B) They may break through to the non-Trump supporters by finding out what binds us rather than what divides us (like the man at the sushi bar for example).

C) They may send a clear message to those who have erred.

So here goes.

Supporting Trump

Did I support Donald Trump for President in 2015 and 2016? You bet I did! Does this mean I do not recognize the flaws in this man? Does this mean I agree with *all* his views and positions? Of course not, and the same goes with most candidates and any President. I have nothing to apologize for here. I know just where I stand and why.

I recognize the unprecedented, relentless attacks and accusations cast upon this one man, Donald Trump (which is a wake-up call all on it's on if you know what I mean), of which an overwhelming majority are twisted, skewed, out of context, completely fabricated, and false. Provide real evidence for me, and then we can discuss it. Until then, grow up and get a life.

To best understand my views of Donald Trump and the Trump phenomenon, I would suggest reading my 2016 book, *"What One Man Can Do"*. It's all in there. This book, *Trump and the Resurrection of America*, picks up where that book left off. My next book will be published in March of 2020 and I will hold nothing back in regards to the subject matter at hand.

In my attempt to effectively and honestly communicate with *anyone* who does not care for President Donald Trump (and that is probably putting it mildly), I would hope that you read this book and find what you *DO* agree with. Is there something perhaps here within the pages of this book that may prove beneficial for you, your family, America, and the world? Is there something within these pages that perhaps you can learn from? Some things that are common to us all – subjects that bind us? Consider this.

Tragedy Brings Unity

Let me ask you a question, okay? What would happen if there were disruptions to the food supply, no access to clean water, or catastrophic natural or man-made disasters? How important will the differences that divide us be then? Would you not help a child in need because his or her parents supported Trump instead of Clinton or vice versa? Ridiculous. Absolutely ridiculous.

I believe people are inherently good. Yes, by some measures, about 20% or more of the global population is problematic and messing things up for not only themselves, but for anyone who crosses their path.

And yes, by some measures there are 2 to 3% who are psychotic, paranoid, sociopaths wreaking havoc (many of whom will be named in this book) and making this a prison planet, but, still, I believe people are instinctively and inherently good.

September 11, 2001

Did anyone in the towers or down on the ground in and around the World Trade Center think for one moment about not saving a person's life or not helping a traumatized hurt person because he or she was black or white? Gay or straight? A Democrat or Republican? Did racism ever cross anyone's mind? I should say not. Why? Because we are *instinctively* and *inherently* good, and we are indeed brothers and sisters united in a much bigger cause and purpose. We are interdependent upon one another. My survival is linked to your survival and vice versa. In moments of sudden tragedy, it is instinctive that we help each other; this is one of the better virtues of the human race. This is love; this is brotherhood. My gosh, when will we ever learn.

Well, over the course of the past twenty-odd years, some family and friends have distanced themselves from me due to my expressed views and their unwillingness to look at these *disruptive, uncomfortable truths* that I speak of. Many of these truths have come to be and are now today shining in bright light for all to see. The test of time has proven me to be right, but still the blissfully ignorant go on about their lives as though it were business as usual. It is not business as usual, and I can assure you of this.

I also spend some time on Facebook (yes, I am aware of all the issues of Facebook and wrote about that in *Misconceptions and Course Corrections*). I spend time on Facebook because I lived abroad mostly and travel frequently, and it is a great way to stay in touch with family and friends all over the world. Without Facebook, the chances of us sharing daily events, staying connected, sharing travel experiences, and such would be minimal, if at all. I also use Facebook to spread the message of my work, my books, consulting, and public speaking. Let me get back on track.

Got Friends?

During the election of 2016, there were family members and friends who began unfollowing me, and then a lifelong friend of over forty years actually unfriended me out of the blue due to the fact that we differed on the candidates for President. A friend of over forty years! And BTW, we never even exchanged any FB chats on the subject of politics. Just the light, fun, friendly things that you often see on FB. This unfriending occurred shortly after I sent him a gift for his retirement. There was also a family member who has known me from birth who, too, unfriended me out of the blue. Truly an amazing time we are living in. This happened after a couple of years of very engaging FB chats with lots of love and admiration being exchanged between us. Oh well, so be it.

It is also noteworthy to mention that I was not a fan of President Obama from the very beginning. I expressed these views as such. Once I learned all about the Bushes (mentioned a bit later on in this book), I expressed my non-favorable views (to put it mildly) about President Bush just as I did about President Obama. But guess what? I did not "unfriend" anyone for the love and support they had/have for BHO, nor did I riot, destroy property, break laws, kill people, and so on.

Can you not see that your actions are the very actions you claim that Trump and his supporters are guilty of, when the truth is, it is you who are guilty of such acts? Can you not see this? It is sad that you cannot. After all, with the drugs, medicines, chemtrails, *entrainment*, corrupt education, mainstream media, and so on, it's a wonder you can even think at all. When you look up the word hypocrite in the dictionary, I am afraid we see your picture. How pathetic. Well, that is a sad commentary for what has become of our country and poor specimens representing the human race and brotherly love. There is much work to be done. So, let's conclude with the "tragedy brings unity" topic. Please read on.

Crisis of Magnitude

We don't need a crisis of magnitude to love each other. Everybody loves you when you're six feet in the ground. Love each other now. If you love freedom and peace, how can you behave this way? Let's take racism as yet another example. Whenever I hear someone side with either the blacks or the whites in a prejudiced or racist tone, I know at once they are part of the problem of the race issue and simply do not get it.

You took the bait and are acting out just as anticipated in the *Hegelian Dialectic,* which I have dedicated a chapter to in this book. What's the Hegelian Dialectic, you say? Find out. Go look it up. Is ignorance really bliss? I also dedicated an entire chapter to race in *Misconceptions and Course Corrections,* what it is, where it comes from, and how it can end.

Divide and Conquer

Division. You see this all over the mainstream news, on the Internet, on Facebook and Twitter, as well as behind closed doors. The only side to be taking is the side of love and unity, period. Funny how the media does not seem to provide that as one of their options. It seems not to be a part of the nightly news narrative.

Funny how that works, isn't it? Can't you see we are being played? How blind and ignorant can people be to simply choose a side *they* offer and then just regurgitate and repeat all the talking points they heard on the nightly news narratives? This makes me sick. Grow a pair! Get a voice, like, how about your own?

By not doing so, you have fallen for the trap, and, in my view, to a greater or lesser extent, you are in fact a part of the problem. How utterly exhausting. Now of course, if a person – regardless of color, political favor, or any other category you would like to pick that dif-ferentiates us – if this person is harming others or breaking the law or transgressing against society, etc., you can choose to have opinions about such a person. But have them for their actions, not for the color of their skin, religion, sexual preference, or political choice. Look at individuals one on one. How do they treat other people? This tells you all you need to know. You may also want to check out some pointed words from Johnathan Gentry.[1]

Conclusion

So, again, on September 11, 2001, did anyone in the towers or down on the ground in and around the World Trade Center think for one moment about not saving a person's life or helping a traumatized, hurt person because he or she was black or white, gay or straight, rich or poor, or in support of a candidate not of your liking? Did these questions cross anyone's mind? I should say not. Why? Because we are instinctively and inherently good,[2] tragedy brings unity, and we are indeed brothers and sisters united in a much bigger cause and purpose. We are dependent upon one another. My survival is linked to your survival and vice versa. In moments of sudden tragedy, it is *instinctive* that we help each other; this is one of the better virtues of the human race. This is love[3]; this is brotherhood. Civilization as we know it is about to change, and tragedy may be at our doorstep. Why wait until then to unite? It may then be too late.

And as to the points where we may differ, I would propose respectable, intelligent discourse between two mature adults to discuss such differences with the hopes we can learn from and inspire each other. At the end, we can always agree to disagree, but let us also focus on what we do agree about. And if you do not wish to return America to being a country governed by the rule of law, a country that will adhere to the U.S. Constitution, the Declaration of Independence, and the Bill of Rights, then I say much of the material in this book you may find challenging to accept. I welcome the challenge.

Having said that, I welcome you aboard just the same. And for you, the lunatic fringe who chooses violence, hate, and crime against

---

1 Johnathan Gentry, https://www.youtube.com/user/johnathangentry
2 https://johnmichaelchambers.com/spiritual-being/
3 https://johnmichaelchambers.com/choose-love/

anyone who disagrees with you, I urge you to come to your senses or simply get out of the way. You will be dealt with later and it may not be pleasant. I will let you figure that one out on your own. You have already taken too much of my time. Like a pack of annoying, barking dogs chasing the fire engine, the fire engine excels forward to put out the real fire, saving your butt as well, although unbeknownst to you. And again, trust me, you will be dealt with later and it may not be pleasant. You have a choice and a decision to make. Choose wisely and be cognizant of your acts. Now that I have gotten that out of the way, let's move on, shall we?

Trump and the Resurrection of America

Many people are not happy with the election of Donald Trump. So be it. Many were not happy with President Obama just the same. The fact is, Trump has restored hope and inspiration for the silent majority, not only in America but across the globe. People who have been oppressed, suppressed, minimalized, and marginalized. But with Trump in office, leadership has come to the forefront, leadership that has been missing for such a very long time, and now the voice of the people has finally been heard.

During the primaries we witnessed the birth of BREXIT, a shock to the ruling elite. And because of Donald Trump and the Trump phenomenon, the globalists, the establishment, the Deep State and the Shadow Government of this world, has experienced its first real threat and setback. And thus the battle begins, as President Donald Trump is leading America's second revolution, trumping global governance. But there is only so much that one man can do.

Unity

History has shown us that one woman or one man can and do make a difference, but not without the overwhelming mass support of the people. We must all come together, now. We must understand, among many other things, that we need to be realistic and know that the establishment is still in place and very much in control at nearly every trigger point. This is beginning to change. True as that may be, in another sense we have the power. The power is within the people. We simply outnumber them, and we are on the right side of history. It is important to understand that the enemies of Donald Trump (and we will touch on this later) are also the enemies of sovereign nations and of freedom itself. They are more evil than you may think, and their intention to rule every aspect of our lives and every resource on this planet has serious, long-lasting, horrific, unimaginable, and unfathomable consequences. Not the kind of world you would like to leave behind to your children or grandchildren.

The Battle Begins

Trump to the New World Order (known today as the Ruling Elite, the Globalists, Deep State, or Global Governance) is an unexpected nuisance, sort of like an annoying mosquito. The problem is mosquitos can easily be done away with. And thus the real battle has just begun.

The masked men and women who once were hiding behind the proverbial curtain of the great and powerful Wizard of Oz have had very little, if any, real opposition or threat from "we the silenced people." Well, not until recently and not until now. They are boldly revealing themselves in broad daylight. You see, they are now "hidden in plain sight." And this tells me the gloves are coming off as it is indeed the eleventh hour.

It is my belief that civilization is at a crossroads. We are at a pivotal stage in a battle between good and evil that has been going on for a millennium. A raised understanding is needed as to the realization that a major paradigm shift is under way and that we have been living in a web of deceitful lies designed to entrap us and move us away from the spirit and more toward vanity, worldly possessions, and servitude as we march blindly like useless idiots down the road to serfdom. Donald Trump, a very unlikely candidate, has risen to heed the call. This is part of the great awakening and, in this, there is true hope.

The challenges we face are enormous, but the scales are tipping. This is our time. We have a chance. The time for action is now. You are nothing more than an accomplice, should you stand by idly, as the culture and planet decline rapidly into a very, very unpleasant condition. I have no hidden agenda here within this body of work. I am not running for office, nor do I plan on running for office. It seems these days I am more of a *political atheist*, (one who realizes that the two-party tyranny system has failed us miserably) if you will. Yes, I am a registered Republican, but right now, it is all about Donald Trump. I am for Trump. I am not asking for your vote. Spiritual as I am and a believer in the supreme being, Religion too is failing us. I am part of no religion. I'm simply just one man stepping out from my "Plan B living semi-retirement in Asia" to chip in and do my part. Allow me to elaborate.

What I am trying to accomplish is to help awaken, inspire, and motivate individuals to rise up and to keep the momentum going while we have this brief moment, this brief breath in eternity to turn the tide. We must focus on what can and should be done, and then be doing it, as talk is cheap. But this requires getting out of comfort zones and applying critical thinking. This requires a bit of sacrifice. Becoming first a truth seeker, then a truth revealer. This requires the ability to not only embrace change, but to create change and then of course be that change. We will need unwavering faith and strength, as this is happening on our watch – we must redirect humanity, if not for our own immediate benefit, at least for posterity. It's by no accident that you are here, and it is quite an exciting time to be alive. Let's take a look at where we are. Let's identify both the dangers and the opportunities and then let's become even more active than perhaps we are right now.

This is no time to be resting on our laurels.

With the recent upset of the century, the shadow government of this world has experienced its first real setback with BREXIT and with the election of Donald J. Trump as President of the United States. The globalists now tremble as Trump and this movement threatens their totalitarianism world government. Although optimism has returned, the battle now begins as President Donald J. Trump leads America's second revolution.

This book picks up where my previous book *"What One Man Can Do"* leaves off. It addresses some very disruptive, uncomfortable truths, yet inspires and empowers the reader like no other body of work on this topic. We must acquire a substantially new way of thinking if we are to win this battle. Failure is not an option. I thank you for coming across this book with the hopes that you will read it, share it, and spread the word. Why? Because everything depends upon what we do right here, right now. Put on your seat belts for my next book in March of 2020 as Trump takes on the Deep State and races towards a Trump 2020 victory!

> *"We must not surrender to the false song of globalism, so I am asking everyone to join this incredible movement. I am asking you to dream big and bold and daring things for your family and for your country."*
>
> *– Donald J. Trump*

When your children and grandchildren ask you, "What were you doing when the global governance was being introduced to America and the world?" what will your answer be? Freedom…it's up to US.

SECTION II: THE WORLD IN WHICH WE LIVE

Exposing the enemy and their agenda

CHAPTER ONE: THE ELECTION THAT WAS NEVER MEANT TO BE

IN MY PREVIOUS BOOK *"WHAT ONE MAN CAN DO"*, I wrote about the Trump phenomenon as it occurred in real time and expressed my views via commentary and analysis of why this election was so critical and how this was (and still is) America's last stand. I truly believe that without the election of Donald J. Trump and with the election of Hillary Clinton, the last nail in the coffin of freedom would have been irrevocably hammered. Thank God this did not happen. Instead, what we got was the election that was never meant to be.

The relentless attacks and assaults on Donald Trump were (and still are) another unprecedented phenomenon exposing who the enemies of not only Donald Trump are, but the enemies of freedom itself. Trump remained focused, worked harder than any other candidates, spent less, played the media like a fiddle, gaining perhaps billions of dollars in media coverage for free, broke scores of records, and became the voice of the people, the first non-politician President of the United States in modern history.

Election Reflection

Like so many others across this nation and perhaps all over the world, I was shocked as we watched the election results on the evening of November 8th.

On one level I knew that Donald Trump would win as was evident from his hugely successful 2015 and 2016 campaign, filling stadiums and arenas in every city and state with thousands of people gathered outside unable to get in. Clinton spoke before groups that typically did not exceed a few hundred people, in addition to having to cancel rallies due to no attendance at all.

My concerns for a Trump loss were based upon the rigged system ensuring a Clinton victory. I am talking about voter fraud and election theft, but Clinton couldn't even win an election that was rigged in her favor. I will discuss some possible ways that Trump out-trumped her in the next chapter. All I can say is much to my surprise Trump won on November 8th and I cannot find words to express how unbelievably happy I was with this outcome – ecstatic and energized. It truly was a surreal moment. So let's take a look at the events that led to the upset of the century, as this is important.

Upset of the Century

With the orchestrated efforts from the evil merchants of chaos (of course I am referring to the political left, much of the Democrat and Republican leadership, Hollywood, the Deep State, and the media, etc.) all in support of Hillary Clinton, Trump persevered and still prevailed. They were stunned. Never throughout our electoral process history has there been such an effort to rail against one candidate. I had written a blog on my blog site[1] during the campaign about the enemies of Trump where I stated that we often judge people by the friends they keep but perhaps also, and even more so, by the enemies we have. So,

---

1   https://johnmichaelchambers.com/

as the shadow government's globalist, tyrannical plans for a police state, one-world government was about to seize complete control with the election of Clinton. America's freedom and the course of the world hung in the balance.

The corrupt psychopaths who own and control the systems that govern this world threw everything they had at Trump. I mean everything. And once again Trump prevailed. Meanwhile they cleverly kept Clinton safeguarded. I mean, after all, there were her questionable health issues on full display for the world to see. Then there was Benghazi, the Clinton Foundation, and the email scandal. Never mind a longstanding record of corruption, flip-flops, and public lies. But the controlled and endlessly funded system managed to keep her alive and free while funding BLM riots and throwing everything they had at Trump and his supporters.

And I sure hope you hard-core Republicans have learned that this is a one-party system serving the same master. The list of Republicans who either did not support Trump, or even worse yet turned on Trump (some overtly and some covertly) should be an eye-opener. From "Low Energy Jeb" (and the whole Bush clan), to Paul Ryan, to lyin' Ted, to "Little Marco" and the list goes on and on and on. This election (among other things) has shown us who the enemies of freedom are. It has shone a light on the rigged and corrupt political system and the bought-and-paid-for, biased media void of true journalism. We must identify our enemies if we are to resurrect America. Not only did they attempt to discredit and destroy Donald Trump and his "deplorables" here at home, but remember, they own and control the majority of the media, so this was global as the international media had a field day with Trump and America as well. This coupled with false, rigged polling to set the expectation for a close race with Clinton in the lead all failed on November 8, 2016.

Trump Victory

Some say the enormous support and prayers from the evangelicals in America helped to elect Trump. Some say it was miraculous and that, by the grace of God, we have been given one more chance in our final hour of need. This may very well be the last lifeline for America, as this is America's last stand.

The American people were catapulted from their oppressed, apathetic, silenced state of mind into action, optimism, and unity thanks to the leadership and true hope and promise from then candidate Donald Trump. Trump became the voice of the silenced people, the movement began, and the Trump phenomenon gained momentum and does to this day globally.

People had caught on to the Obama deception long ago and now they had a larger-than-life voice on the global stage to reflect their views. People knew that if Clinton was elected we would see a continuation of Obama and how his agenda was destructive for America. So people who did not necessarily even like Donald Trump cast their vote for Trump just the same. Senator Bernie Sanders also gained popularity that, I believe, was not expected as well, but he was easily removed simply by stealing his votes through the corrupt voter fraud methods, which will be covered in the next two chapters. Sanders then sold out and buckled. The Clinton clan and the DNC were hard at work doing what they do best: lie, cheat, and steal. But the mostly millennial grassroots opposition to Clinton (the supporters of Sanders), coupled with the supporters of Trump, had one thing in common. They had no jobs.

People came to realize that we had lost our jobs over the past two decades under Clinton, Bush and Obama and due to globalization. People began to realize that with Hillary Clinton in office, these jobs were not returning home. People often vote with their pocketbooks. This was good news for Trump, especially after they stole the opportunity away from Bernie Sanders. This coupled with the increasing awareness that the Clintons were criminals who have (to date) gotten away with multiple felonies and treasonous acts, led to the decision that it was time for true hope and real change. The votes went to Trump!

Thank You, Julian Assange

Although Clinton managed to escape prosecution during the campaign, she did not manage to escape the WikiLeaks reports; thank you, Julian Assange. The onslaught of information released was severely damaging for the Clintons and just at the right time. After all, who wants to vote for a treasonous, criminal, accused occultist pedophile? If Julian Assange makes it into the US courts, I believe we will learn more about the Clinton e-mails, as well as what happened to Seth Rich.

And so the Trump movement spread across America as well as all over the world. People tend to rally behind true leaders, especially where there has been a void for so long. This movement is global and now with Donald Trump in office, we will continue to see increasing numbers of people from all over the world standing up to tyrannical global governance. But the stakes are high and the dangers enormous.

Changing the Narrative

Never underestimate what one man can do. Donald Trump brought all the real issues that matter most to the people to the forefront, and shocked and disrupted the controlled information cartels agenda, thus the relentless attacks. And, at the end of the day, building the wall, tough Muslim deportation and immigration policies, second amendment rights, and more, resonated with the people. Trump won by a landslide, as I forecasted in an earlier blog post in 2016.

Donald Trump changed the controlled programmed narrative with subjects and slogans, such as building the wall, and crushing ISIS, and banning un-vetted Muslims from entering the U.S. He talked about protecting the Second Amendment and bringing jobs back home. He railed against Obamacare and pledged to repeal and replace it. He spoke of the worst deal ever – the Iran deal – and what horrible negotiators we have in these politicians. He explained how TPP will nail the coffin shut for economic opportunity and leverage for the U.S. He spoke of Americanism and Nationalism – America first versus globalism. In essence, he changed the contrived and controlled narrative, *exposing, humiliating,* and *infuriating* the established ruling elite Deep State and Shadow Government. It's a wonder he is alive. I will discuss *that* subject a bit further on in this book.

Trump brought to the forefront how our military is depleted and how our vets are not taken care of once they return home. He spoke of the corrupt, rigged political system and the biased, corrupt, lying media. He talked about the destructive ways of political correctness, and how we have no time for such nonsense. He warned of a serious market correction and a deep recession that is looming. And all throughout the campaign, the people began in unison shouting, "Build that wall! Build that wall!" Then Trump would ask… "And who is going to pay for it?" "Mexico," the people replied. Also, there was chanting all across America referring to the three-time loser (in one election), criminal Clinton, by saying, "Lock her up, lock her up." Now that is changing the narrative. Never underestimate what one man can do.

Summary

And so, with the election that was never meant to be, perhaps for the first time, Deep State and the Shadow Government has been threatened and has suffered a serious setback to the agenda they have been hard at work on this for decades thanks in no small part to Donald Trump. Never underestimate what one man can do.

And now we have this chance to resurrect America as President Trump leads the second American revolution. We must unite with one heart and one mind and expand this circle across America and then across the globe. President Trump needs your support. For we are America. Optimism returns, but the battle begins. The torch has now been passed.

I wrote this song back in 1999–2000 titled "We Are America." (I guess you might say I was like Panasonic, "just slightly ahead of my time.") The song can be listened to on my YouTube[2] channel. I added the lyrics to this book as I believe it is apropos to the message at hand. The lyrics are provided here below.

We Are America

Johnny was a friend of mine although I did not know him long. Looked into his eyes and he was gone. Making no mistake, knowing what's at stake, he came back to this place. A place called America. The rays of light and love are shining down upon thee. Johnny was a friend of mine although I did not know him long. Looked into his eyes and he was gone. We are free; we are America. We are free; we are America.

He was a working man doing the best he can, trying to find his way through. Realized the divine plan, cried out for every man; yes, the hour is at hand. Johnny was a friend of mine although I did not know him long. Looked into his eyes and he was gone. We are free; we are America. We are free; we are America. We are free; we are America. We are free; we are America.

And now it's up to me, freedom for eternity, to carry this torch which has been passed. The light of a thousand suns shines down on everyone. It's the light of God that never fails. Johnny was a friend of mine although I did not know him long. Looked into his eyes and he was gone.

---

2   https://www.youtube.com/watch?v=9vjD-J4A3MQ&index=3&list=PLEXgzPtAt
FJm8_uM13gjzpityMJ2AfsD

Feel it in your heart, sing, "America I AM, oh, America I AM." Forever embraced by the rainbow of light and love. "Oh, America I AM." The light expanding in America. The light protecting America. Awaken now, the choice is yours. Oh, World Victorious!

We are free; we are America. We are free; we are America. And you know it's so true. We are free; we are America. We are free; we are America. And the light it shines through. We are free; we are America.

CHAPTER TWO: FREE AND FAIR ELECTIONS

AMERICANS ARE UNDER THE ILLUSION that there is a two-party system in place and that we have free and fair elections and we have a choice. But, in actuality, it really is a one-party system serving the same master. I will get into this in the chapter titled "Shadow Government." Let's discuss the U.S. free and fair elections. Free and fair elections? Oh really? Ask Donald Trump and Bernie Sanders about free and fair elections.

The United States actually has the worst voting system in the developed world. According to NYU professor Mark Crispin Miller, even Harvard University ranked the U.S. dead last place in the developed world. Professor Miller went on to say that former President Jimmy Carter said in 2006 in an NPR interview that the elections in the U.S. are so poor that we don't even rise to the minimal level where the Carter Center would bother to monitor them.

You see, we are under the illusion that we have free and fair elections when, in fact, the candidates are "selected," funded with full-blown support from the PACS, big corporations, the corrupt, biased media, and then placed into office. We have shed blood across this globe, fighting for others to have the right to free and fair elections, yet we do not. It is "they" who get to decide who becomes the President of the United States. Well, that all changed with the election of Donald J. Trump in 2016, being perhaps the only exception in modern history. Consider this.

Voter Fraud and Election Theft

Voter fraud and election theft have been going on for a very long time and perhaps even more so today. Who is guilty? Well, both parties are guilty; depends upon what the shadow government's agenda is.

We see reports where dead people are voting. During the primaries of 2016, absentee ballots were seen being shredded into a waste basket.

Why is it that with the majority of the contested recounts we mostly find tens of thousands of missing ballots for the Democrats and not the Republicans? I mean, what are the odds of that? Slim I would suggest, slim. Am I insinuating that there is voter fraud and election theft taking place in Florida and other states as well? You bet. Now, there is plenty of news out there about the recounts taking place that can be found on social media and by scouring the various news feeds, so I will not regurgitate.

There is gerrymandering taking place as yet another method. There are instances where one person has voted multiple times. There is the corruption in play with the PACS that Donald Trump spoke out against during the primaries of 2015 and 2016. Some years ago, in the Tampa Bay area of Florida, there were sworn affidavits which have been collected by a team spearheaded by attorney Mark Adams,[1] indicating that votes were significantly changed in local elections, not to mention the onslaught of illegal aliens voting. There are many other instances of fraud, but perhaps the most telling and most disturbing

1 Mark Adams, https://www.youtube.com/watch?v=8kdnq8XZ_BQ

one of all is the fact that the Diebold voting machines are hackable and rigged.[2] Then there is the process known as "skimming."[3] What is skimming?

Skimming

- » A very sophisticated method of election fraud.
- » The most common way to "steal" an election.
- » Manipulate pre-election polls to project a "close race".
- » Design the polls to have a wide margin of error.
- » Wide margins rig the system against any effective legal challenge.
- » Manipulate the vote to make sure the race is close.
- » Fit the official vote to hide within the black hole (i.e., margin of error).
- » Skimming is hard to detect and almost impossible to prove.
- » Honest campaigns can only win in real landslides of 10% or more, unless a scientific polling technology could be deployed that generates cost-effective, statistically robust results with very small margin of error.

Traditional Polling

So, with typical polling, you see often a "select" group of people being polled. The number of people being polled is typically five hundred to two thousand and then, with traditional polling, you can expect a margin of error to be as high as 6 to 10%. This is about as effective as polling a group of steak eaters at a large steak house in one neighborhood and asking them if they prefer steak or seafood for dinner. This is the same method used in political polling. This type of polling is not representative of the electorate across the country, and so the fix is in,

2 Programmer Under Oath Admits Computers Rig Elections, https://www.youtube.com/watch?v=G0qivPudp6U
3 Election Fraud and Skimming – Can it be prevented? https://www.youtube.com/watch?v=UWdvU5zOw7Y&list=PLIiFq_bi5oLjnmAWJuQ8iYipRXCJ0YzQo

and the expectation is set, and the biased media's talking points set the narrative for the regurgitating puppets, we the "sheeple."

For example, after the second debate between Donald Trump and Hillary Clinton, CNN released a poll minutes after the debate, a select group of people totaling just 537, and the poll resulted in Hillary beating Trump 57 to 34% in that debate. CNN reported that 58% of those polled were democrats.

Anyone who watched, even Hillary supporters, knows that Trump slaughtered her in this particular debate. I rest my case. Skewed, rigged polling, skimming the elections. The plot thickens.

Edison Research Group

What is the Edison Research Group[4]? This group conducts the exit poll results on election day. They provide the data under an exclusive contract to the National Election Pool (a cartel of six huge media conglomerates: ABC, CBS, CNN, FOX, NBC, and AP). Edison is owned by the same six cartel members. How cozy and convenient. And with the GEMS manipulation capabilities in place and if the artificial intelligence (AI) is activated, election theft occurs. Think about it, private for-profit companies tell us about our election results outcome. Are you hearing me? Are you following me? Are you with me so far?

All of the mainstream media (MSM) and now, as recently observed, even some of the alternative media will never get into the crux of the voter fraud and election theft issue. Sure they might touch on the dead voters, the voter who has voted more than once, and so on, but preprogrammed computers with AI? You probably won't hear that on the MSM. Discussing computerized election fraud is generally off limits. It's like discussing how the twin towers came down on 911, not to mention building number seven.[5] These subjects are off limits when it comes to MSM, and so the blackout and gag order are in full force

---

4 http://www.edisonresearch.com/election-polling/
5 WTC Building 7 Collapse, https://www.youtube.com/watch?v=JnLcUxV1dPo

and Americans are once again hoodwinked and a laughingstock to the world.

GEMS

The GEMS[6] resident software had been installed on virtually all central server voting machines deployed in the U.S. and can easily steal the election, undetected, with extreme precision. This is also known as black box voting.[7] There is some evidence that this technology was used by Hillary to steal her primary from Senator Sanders.[8] The GEMS software has now been placed under the control of an advanced Artificial Intelligence system that can continuously manipulate the "official vote" tally nationwide in nanoseconds, right down to the precinct level, without detection. This system will have been specifically designed and *purpose-built* to be the perfect tool – leaving no evidence behind – in order to commit the perfect crime.

WikiLeaks has provided credible evidence that the pre-election presidential polls were being rigged [9] as well, in order to set the expectation for a Clinton victory. Meanwhile, Clinton and Kaine had been canceling rallies due to little to no attendance as Trump continued to fill arenas across the nation, with thousands more lined up outside unable to get in.

Enough said. So how did Trump win? Counter AI was deployed, in the nick of time thus preventing the theft, ensuring the victory for Trump. We do know that the election process in America is fatally flawed for multiple reasons and Russia as we all know, had nothing to do with this.

6 Fraction Magic Short Version, https://www.youtube.com/watch?v=8ezmpqwVEnM&feature=youtu.be
7 Fraction Magic – Part 1: Votes are being counted as fractions instead of as whole numbers, http://blackboxvoting.org/fraction-magic-1/
8 BREAKING: Evidence Clinton Foundation "Paid Off" Voting Machine Companies, STOLE PRIMARY, https://conservativedailypost.com/
9 New Podesta Email Exposes Playbook For Rigging Polls Through "Oversamples," http://www.zerohedge.com/news/2016-10-23/new-podesta-email-exposes-dem-playbook-rigging-polls-through-oversamples

Forward Progress

"The people who cast the votes don't decide an election, the people who count the votes do."

– Joseph Stalin

The Founding Fathers stated the votes are to be cast in private and counted in public. This of course is no longer being done since the advent of computerized voting. Think about it – have you ever seen a computer count? The following suggestions regarding an overhaul to our flawed corrupt election process were made by NYU Professor Mark Crispin Miller.[10]

» Eliminate private companies with vested interests in the counting and reporting of votes.
» Return to hand-counted paper ballots.
» Get rid of computerized voting.
» Require automatic registration on birthdays.
» Election Day should be a national holiday.

These, in my opinion, are sound and simple steps to take to help restore election integrity. There is another method, yet another way of detecting and deterring voter fraud and election theft.

PollMole

You may recall in my open letter at the beginning of this book that I mentioned I spent some time assisting with a startup company leading up to the election of 2016. That company was PollMole. So, what is PollMole, you may ask? Reminds me of the movie *Back to the Future*, where the guy says to Marty, "Who the hell is JFK?" This may soon become the case with PollMole. Time will tell.

---

10 Mark Crispin Miller: Can U.S. Elections Really Be Stolen? Yes. https://www.youtube.com/watch?v= NxXKr2hKCz0&feature=youtu.be

PollMole is a highly disruptive, transformative social networking and connectivity technology. It empowers its users to directly and interactively retrieve, analyze, process, archive, and share opinions, ideas, beliefs, and other forms of complex information, from an almost unlimited number of people, simultaneously, in real time, twenty-four/ seven, and translate this information into actionable intelligence, thus providing extremely accurate, focused, science-based information designed to optimize the decision-making ability.

Whew. So, how does this relate to the election process? In essence, PollMole bypasses the traditional content controls erected by the big media's information cartel and delivers real information directly into the hands of we the people. PollMole is a downloadable app that can help to restore election integrity results. When you download your free app and cast your anonymous vote, an electronic affidavit is registered within the technological platform. Should there be an election contest, PollMole can become quite the useful tool as a "weapon of truth" if you will.

If a court order was presented to PollMole, the candidate contesting the election outcome might find PollMole most useful. After all, if there were a large sampling of votes cast across all 180,000+ precincts, say, with twenty million votes having been casted and recorded in the PollMole app with a near zero margin of error, this would detect just where the voter fraud took place and perhaps reveal enough forensic evidence to overturn the election results. This would be historical and a real game changer. In fact, this would change everything.

In addition to detecting voter fraud and election theft, there would be consequences, such as prosecution, for those who committed the fraud. This can be widespread as you move up and down the channels.

Furthermore, the media and the rigged polling organizations, agencies, and corporations, as well as the pundits, are caught with their pants down, exposed and discredited, and so the media itself must then become honest and straight or simply lose their audience, ratings, and revenues.

And due to the way the firewalls have been constructed within the PollMole back-end technology, the names of those who cast the votes remain anonymous as intended by the Founding Fathers.

You can learn more about this startup company called PollMole by visiting the company's developing website[11] and by doing a Google search. The founder, my friend Dr. Richard Davis, has since passed on. The company still exists and is under restructure at this time.

President Trump has been talking about the importance of having paper ballots as a back-up to the computers and rightly so. The Founding Fathers stated the votes are to be cast in private and counted in public. Has anyone ever seen a computer count? I would submit to you that with the advent of computerized vote tabulation, that our voting process is in fact unconstitutional.

---

11 http://www.pollmole.vote/

CHAPTER THREE: SHADOW GOVERNMENT

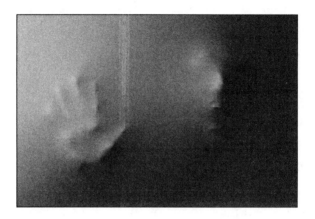

THERE IS A SYSTEM IN PLACE, a clandestine, sophisticated network that controls the world we live in. It creates the narrative that permeates throughout the world and becomes the false reality we have all come to know as our way of life. Our civilization is entering the beginning stages of a major collision, and a much-needed course correction is in order. President Trump and we the people must meet this challenge. Failure is not an option.

Psychopaths & Sociopaths

The world is run by insane people with insane objectives. These individuals are living in a chronic state of fear and believe that everyone is a threat to them and to their very survival. They are crazy. They seek to dominate. They seek absolute control over every aspect of our lives. They seek to suppress and to destroy. They are warmongers and dictators. Many of the men are dressed in expensive business suits and the women in expensive pant suits. Unlike most of the human race, they carry out their acts with absolutely no conscience whatsoever as they are deranged and detached from the light of God to such an extent that evil permeates through them. You should know by now who these individuals are, and, if you don't, you will be able to identify them soon, once you come to learn about *False Flag Operations, Problem-Reaction-Solution,* and the *Hegelian Dialectic,* as these will be addressed later on in this book.

These psychopaths and sociopaths are hard to detect, as they are intelligent, clever, artful, and often rise to positions of power. Many of these individuals are sexual deviants, pedophiles, and belong to demonic groups as recently released by WikiLeaks. They are very manipulative and have seized power and control over every aspect of our lives, our speech, and even our thoughts. They have infiltrated and corrupted our education system, health-care system, religious institutions, the media, and most forms of entertainment. They have seized control over and poisoned our food supply and all natural resources. Yes, it is this shadow government that controls the world in which we live, making Earth and its inhabitants prisoners on a prison planet. Now, please don't shoot me, I am only the messenger. So, how do they do this?

The Big Club

They formed, own, and control the "big club" and, like the comedian George Carlin[1] said (very strong language in the Carlin link), "You and me, we ain't in it." We are nothing more than pawns on the chessboard of life being used as they so choose. They think of us and describe us as useless eaters. So, who is part of the big club? The big club can be described as an intricate, interconnected web of organizations, corporations, religions, and governments, mostly made up of unelected leaders, many of whom are inbred.

---

1 George Carlin, https://www.youtube.com/watch?v=cKUaqFzZLxU

"No matter how paranoid or conspiracy-minded you are, what the government is doing is worse than you imagine."
– William Blum (former U.S. State Dept. employee)

Again, this is not an all-inclusive chart but it covers the basics. In my opinion the Bilderberg Group in particular will be an integral part of orchestrating the next great financial and economic catastrophe perhaps early on in Donald Trump's Presidency.

Illuminati and Satanic Groups

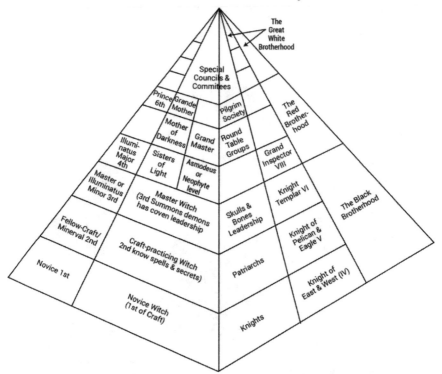

This is a basic (not all-inclusive chart). It boggles the mind that many of our Presidents have come through the "Skull and Bones" society as featured above. I would also encourage you to research "Bohemian Grove." With the recent reports from Julian Assange and WikiLeaks it's no wonder Hilary Clinton could not get elected.

"Many of the conspiracy theories of yesterday have become the conspiracy facts and realities of today."

CHAPTER FOUR: MONEY AND THE FEDERAL RESERVE

THE FEDERAL RESERVE IS A PRIVATE for-profit banking cartel and, although enacted into law in 1913, is in fact unconstitutional. The Federal Reserve is no more a government agency than Federal Express. There is nothing Federal about it and there is no Reserve.

> *"Give me control of a nation's money supply, and I care not who makes its laws."*
>
> *— Amschel Rothschild, mayor, German banker, and founder of the Rothschild family international banking dynasty.*

Formation of the Fed

In November of 1910, on Jekyll Island, Georgia, seven men who represented directly or indirectly one-fourth of the world's wealth met in secrecy for nine days. It is there, at this location, where the charter of the Federal Reserve was drafted. You can visit this now popular tourist site should you find yourself in the state of Georgia.

The Federal Reserve is a privately held for-profit corporation, a banking cartel. The main objective for a corporation is to make a profit, and they do indeed make a profit. Let's take a brief stroll through history as we look into the formation of the Federal Reserve and the results of the Federal Reserve Charter that was enacted into law by the U.S. Congress in 1913.

J.P. Morgan, Senator Nelson Aldrich, Piatt Andrews, Frank Vanderlip, Henry P. Davison, Paul Warburg, and Charles D. Norton arranged for hundreds of millions of dollars to be poured into the campaigns of the most powerful members of Congress. In 1912, they backed an obscure Princeton professor for President of the United States by the name of Woodrow Wilson. He later became President. *The* book to read on this subject is *The Creature from Jekyll Island*[1] by G. Edward Griffin. Get a copy today, read it, share it.

Clandestine Congressional Vote

Late on Tuesday, December 23, 1913, just days after the Christmas recess had commenced, a secret Senate vote was "arranged" with only a few senators remaining in Washington D.C. The act passed with forty-three voting "yea" and twenty-five voting "nay." Twenty-seven did not vote since they had not been notified and had already left town to go home for the holidays. All had previously expressed their opposition to the act. So, on December 23, 1913, their plan worked, one of the most cunning manipulations in parliamentary history; Congress passed the Federal Reserve Act of 1913. In its charter, the act clearly states as its main objective: "To provide the action with a safer, more flexible, and more stable monetary and financial system."

---

1 http://www.amazon.com/The-Creature-Jekyll-Island-Federal/dp/091298645X

Fractional Reserve Lending

This means that a fractional reserve debt system, controlled by a private for-profit corporation, has not worked out too well for the American people and thus, the world to a greater or lesser extent. Challenging the Fed, I mean any real, credible threat placed before this cartel, comes with consequences. It has been said that perhaps one of the main reasons JFK was assassinated was due to his move to end the Fed by returning the U.S. dollar to be backed, not only by gold (as it was then), but also by silver. President Kennedy put forth Executive Order 11110[2] and, some months later, his brains ended up splattered all over his wife's lap.

As we fast-forward to recent history, the invasions of Iraq, Libya, and Syria and the executions of Saddam Hussein and Muammar Gaddafi are highly suspect. These countries did not have a Rothschild's bank and these nations were positioning to decouple from the U.S. petrodollar, creating their own gold-backed currency and, as Madame Hillary said with regards to the killing of Gaddafi, "We came, we saw, he died."[3]

So, did the Fed meet its objectives over the past 104 years? I shall say not! We do not have a more stable monetary financial system at all. What we have is a debt-based monetary system no longer backed by gold or silver with runaway inflation and a devalued currency. We have digital debt. We have a currency that may very well soon be replaced as the world's reserve currency. The federal debt alone exceeds nineteen trillion dollars. It is mathematically impossible to pay off this debt, which will soon reach $22 trillion and more. A "yuge" challenge for incoming President Donald Trump is facing him front and center.

Therefore "a safer, more flexible, and more stable monetary and

2 https://en.wikipedia.org/wiki/Executive_Order_11110
3 Hillary Clinton "We Came, We Saw, He Died" (Gaddafi), https://www.youtube.com/watch?v=FmIRYvJQeHM

financial system" as set forth in this charter clearly has not worked out so well and so, by this means of fractional reserve banking, governments may, secretly and unobserved, confiscate the wealth of the people, and not one man in a million will detect the theft.

This system of fractional reserve banking and the printing of all this fiat (now digital fiat) currency is purely inflationary, and the U.S. dollar has lost over 95% of its purchasing power since its inception. The USA Debt Clock[4] is a real-time calculator reflecting the federal debt of the United States of America. It is a link on the web that you should bookmark.

They unleash what is now digital fiat currency with no tangible backing or accountability into the banking system, and this is then leveraged by fractional reserve banking. The banks then loan out these dollars (with a multiplier of ten or one hundred or more times the amount than they received from the Fed) to other banks, governments, corporations, and individuals and charge an interest rate.

They typically own titles, as in a mortgage or a car loan, and, when they decide to "reap the harvest," they seize the assets when the consumer is unable to survive in a jobless, inflationary climate (which they helped to create). Think 2008.

They also fund both sides of all wars for huge profits as the innocent little children[5] are laid in shallow graves and billed as nothing more than "collateral damage." Fractional reserve banking is also defined in great detail in a simple, easy-to-understand format in the DVDs "Money as Debt"[6] and "The Money Masters,"[7] which can also be viewed on YouTube.

4 http://www.usdebtclock.org/
5 Yusuf – The Little Ones (Live Yusuf's Cafe Session 2007) + Lyrics, https://www.youtube.com/watch?v=2O6_2fvhG0s
6 http://www.moneyasdebt.net/
7 http://www.themoneymasters.com/

U.S. Constitution

This Federal Reserve Act of 1913, although passed by Congress, was in contradiction to the United States Constitution.[8] In Article 1, Section 8, Phrase 5, it clearly states that "Congress shall have power to coin money, regulate the value thereof, and of foreign coin, and fix the standard of weights and measures." This power was given to a private for-profit bank called the Federal Reserve in 1913. Former Congressman, Ron Paul, and now Senator Rand Paul have drafted bills to audit the Fed[9] and sadly, to date, with no success. Perhaps in a Trump administration we will see the end of the Fed. But caution, the last President to try to restore sound money and do away with the Federal Reserve system via Executive Order 11110[10] was gunned down in Dallas. RIP, JFK. God forbid this should ever happen again.

Collapse of the U.S. Petrodollar

I believe the U.S. dollar may experience a false sense of stability for the short to near term, but once the U.S. dollar loses its world reserve currency status, the dollar may collapse and a new currency may be ushered in. The new world currency. This may happen sooner rather than later. Trump is beginning to take on the IMF, the Federal Reserve and the Rothschild Central Banking system, restoring sound money and restoring power to the people. I will go into this in great detail in my next book.

An eye-opening documentary from some years back by the late film producer Aaron Russo is a must-watch for those who are just becoming aware of the subject of the Federal Reserve system. This documentary, *Freedom to Fascism*,[11] can be viewed on YouTube.

---

8 http://www.usconstitution.net/const.html#A1Sec8
9 https://www.congress.gov/bill/114th-congress/senate-bill/264
10 http://www.presidency.ucsb.edu/ws/?pid=59049
11 Aaron Russo's Documentary "America Freedom To Fascism," https://www.youtube.com/watch?v=ZKeaw7HPG04

U.S. Federal Debt Hits $22 Trillion

U.S. Federal debt at the time of this writing exceeds $22,000,000,000. Congratulations to the "Demicans" and Republicrats" and of course to the Fed, and to the ruling elite. The United States is the largest debtor nation in the world. Approximately every two minutes that goes by, the Federal debt alone rises by another million U.S. dollars. Economists, mathematicians, and history tell us this will not have a good ending. President Trump is now taking this on. The restoration of sound money, moving away from a Central Bank based and controlled economy, to restoring power to the people with a gold backed currency. The beginning stages of the Global Financial Reset has now begun.

CHAPTER FIVE: LESSONS FROM THE DUSTBIN OF HISTORY

President Abraham Lincoln

"The government should create, issue, and circulate all the currency and credit needed to satisfy the spending power of the government and the buying power of the consumers. The privilege of creating and issuing money is not only the supreme prerogative of government, but it is the government's greatest creative opportunity."

President Thomas Jefferson

"If the American people ever allow private banks to control the issuance of their currency, first by inflation and then by deflation, the banks and corporations that will grow up around them will deprive the people of all their property until their children will wake up homeless on the continent their fathers conquered."

Amschel Rothschild

(Mayor and German banker. Founder of the Rothschild
family international banking dynasty.)

*"Give me control of a nation's money supply, and I care not who
makes its laws."*

Congressman Charles A. Lindbergh Sr.

*"This Federal Reserve Act establishes the most gigantic trust
on earth. When President Wilson signs this bill, the invisible
government of the monetary power will be legalized. This is the
worst legislative crime of the ages that has been perpetuated by
this banking and currency bill. From now on, all depressions
will be scientifically created."*

President Woodrow Wilson

(After signing the Federal Reserve into existence)

*"I am a most unhappy man. I have unwittingly ruined my coun-
try. A great industrial nation is controlled by its system of
credit. Our system of credit is concentrated. The growth of the
nation, therefore, and all our activities, are in the hands of a
few men. We have come to be one of the worst ruled, one of the
most completely controlled and dominated Governments in the
civilized world, no longer a Government by free opinion, no
longer a Government by conviction and the vote of the majority, but a Government by the opinion and duress of a small
group of dominant men."*

Vladimir Lenin

(Chairman of Russia's Council of People's Commissars 1917–1924)

"The best way to destroy the capitalist system is to debauch its currency. The best way to crush the bourgeoisie (middle class) is to grind them between the millstones of taxation and inflation."

John Maynard Keynes

(Fabian socialist and father of Keynesian Economics)

"By a continuing process of inflation, government can confiscate, secretly and unobserved, an important part of the wealth of their citizens."

G. Edward Griffin

(American author, researcher, and filmmaker)

"Inflation has now been institutionalized at a fairly constant 5%per year. This has been determined to be the optimum level for generating the most revenue without causing public alarm."

Robert Reich

(22nd U.S. Labor Secretary)

"The dirty little secret is that both houses of Congress are irrelevant. Both houses of Congress are now being run by Alan Greenspan and the Federal Reserve, and America's foreign policy is now being run by the IMF. When the President decides

to go to war, he no longer needs a declaration of war from Congress."

And remember, those who fail to learn from history are destined to repeat it, so let's see what happens in this new administration with the Audit the Fed Bill #264.[1]

Meanwhile, tick-tock, tick-tock. USA debt clock.[2]

1 https://www.congress.gov/bill/114th-congress/senate-bill/264/text
2 http://usadebtclock.com/

CHAPTER SIX: GLOBAL GOVERNANCE AND THE NEW WORLD ORDER

GLOBAL GOVERNANCE IS ABOUT POWER AND CONTROL over everything, including life itself. These tyrannical psychopaths are, in fact, the shadow government, weaving their web of chaos and destruction. They use the front groups, treaties, institutions, and governments they established, as well as the puppets they put in place to man these. Puppets like the Bushes, Obama, Merkel, Clinton, Blake and Trudeau, to name but a few. It is not Israel; it is not the U.S., Russia, or China. It is not any identifiable government. It is this shadow government and its henchman and accomplices who are the enemies of freedom. These are our true enemies. Know your enemy well.

They poison our food, air, land, and water. They who force dangerously laced vaccinations on us and rain toxic heavy metals down on us from the sky (geo-engineering/chemtrails[1]). It is they who build nuclear power plants on top of earthquake faults and in tsunami zones.

---

1 G. Edward Griffin Talks Candidly About Chemtrails/SAG, https://www.youtube.com/watch?v=rsWpSPBwA-w

They (as recently released by WikiLeaks) are satanic pedophiles. They start and fund all wars. They murder, rape, and pillage with no conscience and without consequence. They violate laws, racking up scores of felonies by keeping vital secrets of a nation on a private server in the bathroom with no firewall or security of any kind, yet escape justice. We must know who our enemy is and label them. We must not permit our enemy to define for us who our enemy is, as this is a diversion. This is divide and conquer.

Due to the rising awareness of the New World Order and its objectives to control every aspect of our lives, they have gradually, over the years, changed the name and are now better known as globalism or global governance. Sure sounds nice, but make no mistake about it, the New World Order is in full force, and so, meet the new boss – same as the old boss. Remember this announcement from "Papa Bush"? This is a very short video clip of the then President, George Herbert Walker Bush, telling the American people about the stated goal and implementation of the New World Order.[2] The military tribunal of George Herbert Walker Bush will be discussed in detail in my next book.

Watch the clip. Share it on social media with those who call you a conspiracy theorist. Well, that vision of a NWO is here and almost completely implemented, up until now. There is a chance that we can begin to reverse this dwindling spiral but not without a battle, a deadly serious battle at that. I will address this battle in another section of this book.

Global governance is aimed at controlling every aspect of our lives, whether it's financial through the World Bank, the Federal Reserve, the Central Bank, International Monetary Fund, or the large intergovernmental institutions like the United Nations, World Health Organization, and World Trade Organization, which are pushing Agenda 21 and Agenda 2030 to end property rights for everyone and

2 George H.W. Bush New World Order Speech, https://www.youtube.com/watch?v=oN-flYaXNLQ

push us into nationless states. They are pushing the growth of NATO and a supranational military organization. The government is out of control, and that's all a part of global governance.

National sovereignty is falling apart. We can see it happening all over the world. Throughout the world, national sovereignty structures are crumbling under a global governance push and this is why they threw everything they had at Donald Trump in an attempt to prevent his election. They failed. Why? God is on our side, that's why. We operate from within the light with love and compassion. We are dealing with good, not evil and truth, not lies. We are on the right side of history.

So, what are we up against? What are the stated goals of global governance and the new world order? To summarize this in broad and simple terms, the new world order's stated goals is for a one-world government, a one-world military, a one-world justice system, and a one-world currency. President GH Walker Bush expressed this numerous times while in office, which can be viewed on YouTube today.

Through various aspects of their eugenics programs,[3] their desire is to reduce world population from 7.4 billion to approximately 500,000[4] million people. There are many treaties, organizations, executive orders, and bills passed, and in place, that have made significant progress towards achieving the above NWO stated goals. And for those who still consider this to be conspiratorial, I suggest you do your due diligence. There are also many links and sources within this body of work that may be a good starting point. I will delve into the dangers of 5G and how this relates to this topic in my next book.

One of the leading globalists, David Rockefeller, in his book *Memoirs,* admits secretly conspiring for a NWO. In this book, he admits he is part of a secret cabal working to destroy the United States

---

3 Bill Gates: World needs fewer people, http://www.wnd.com/2012/08/
    bill-gates-world-needs-fewer-people/
4 Population control to 500 million https://www.infowars.com/from-7-billion-people-to-500-million-
    people-%E2%80%93-the-sick-population-control-agenda-of-the-global-elite/

and create a new world order. "Some even believe we [Rockefeller family] are part of a secret cabal working against the best interests of the United States, characterizing my family and me as 'internationalists' and of conspiring with others around the world to build a more integrated global political and economic structure – One World, if you will. If that's the charge, I stand guilty, and I am proud of it" (page 405). Also, an important discussion between the late film producer Aaron Russo and Alex Jones on Rockefeller can be viewed on YouTube – "Freedom to Fascism".

Let us not forget the evil Nazi collaborator, currency manipulator, and billionaire, George Soros. Here is a partial transcript from an interview done by Steve Kroft for CBS' *60 Minutes* with George Soros on December 20, 1998.

Kroft: No feeling of guilt?

Mr. Soros: No.

Kroft: For example, that "I'm Jewish and here I am, watching these people go. I could just as easily be there. I should be there." None of that?

Mr. Soros: Well, of course I c–I could be on the other side or I could be the one from whom the thing is being taken away. But there was no sense that I shouldn't be there, because that was—well, actually, in a funny way, it's just like in markets—that if I weren't there—of course, I wasn't doing it, but somebody else would—would—would be taking it away anyhow. And it was the—whether I was there or not, I was only a spectator, the property was being taken away. So the—I had no role in taking away that property. So I had no sense of guilt.

Soros has ownership in many companies and funds many groups and organizations that wreak havoc on the United States and many other places in the world today – companies like Diebold, with the hackable rigged computers used in our election process, as well as funding Black Lives Matter (a domestic terror organization) and media matters. The list goes on and on. You could write a twelve-volume set of books and barely cover the number of treaties, TPP, organizations, and executive orders that are bringing humanity to the cliff's edge. This would include bills which have been passed by a corrupt, complicit, and complacent two-party (e-hum) Congress over the past couple of decades. Let's look at just a bit more before we move on to another topic. You mean you have not yet heard of Agenda 2030? Oh boy.

CHAPTER SEVEN: AGENDA 2030

THE FOLLOWING CONTENT WAS TAKEN FROM the McAlvany Intelligence Advisor[1] October 2015 issue. I encourage you to subscribe to this valuable monthly newsletter well into its fourth decade of publishing.

The United Nations has announced a new global plan for 2030 that will end human freedom under the claimed label of "sustainability." It is actually a plan rooted in government coercion and the crushing of individual freedom. This is the blueprint for a global police state that's being pushed under the claim of "sustainability." (And yes, they will criminalize rainwater collection, home gardening, and homeschooling, too.)

The UN's "2030 Agenda" document being unveiled in late September 2015[2] is being touted as a blueprint for so-called "sustainable development" around the world, but the reality is that this

document describes nothing less than a global government takeover

---

1 https://mcalvanyintelligenceadvisor.com
2 Transforming our world: the 2030 Agenda for Sustainable Development, https://sustainabledevelopment.un.org/post2015/transformingourworld

of every nation across the planet. The "goals" of this document are nothing more than code words for a corporate government fascist agenda that will imprison humanity in a devastating cycle of poverty, while enriching the world's most powerful globalist corporations like Monsanto and DuPont.

To understand the real goals of the 2030 Agenda you have to understand how globalists disguise their monopolistic agendas in "feel good" language.

It should be noted that nowhere does this document state that "achieving human freedom" is one of its goals, and nor does it explain how these goals are to be achieved. The reality is that every single point in this UN agenda is to be achieved through centralized government control and totalitarian mandates that resemble communism

United Nations Agenda 2030

Stated Goal #1: End poverty in all its forms everywhere.
Hidden Reality: Put everyone on government welfare, food stamps, housing subsidies, and handouts that make them obedient slaves to global government.

Never allow people upward mobility to help themselves. Instead, teach mass victimization and obedience to a government that provides monthly "allowance" money for basic essentials like food and medicine. Label it "ending poverty."

Stated Goal #2: End hunger, achieve food security and improved nutrition, and promote sustainable agriculture.
Hidden Reality: Invade the entire planet with GMOs and Monsanto's patented seeds while increasing the use of deadly herbicides under the false claim of "increased output" of food crops. Engineer genetically modified plants to boost specific vitamin chemicals while having no idea of the long-term consequences of genetic pollution or cross-

species genetic experiments carried out openly in a fragile ecosystem.

Stated Goal #3: Ensure healthy lives and promote wellbeing for all at all ages.

Hidden Reality: Mandate 100+ vaccines for all children and adults at gunpoint, threatening parents with arrest and imprisonment if they refuse to co-operate. Push heavy medication use on children and teens while rolling out "screening" programs. Call mass medication "prevention" programs and claim they improve the health of citizens.

Stated Goal #4: Ensure inclusive and equitable quality education and promote lifelong learning opportunities for all.

Hidden Reality: Push a false history and a dumbed-down education under "Common Core" education standards that produce obedient workers rather than independent thinkers. Never let people learn real history, or else they might realize they don't want to repeat it.

Stated Goal #5: Achieve gender equality and empower all women and girls.

Hidden Reality: Criminalize Christianity, marginalize heterosexuality, demonize males, and promote the LGBT agenda everywhere. The real goal is never "equality" but rather the marginalization and shaming of anyone who expresses any male characteristics whatsoever.

The ultimate goal is to feminize society, creating widespread acceptance of "gentle obedience" along with the self-weakening ideas of communal property and "sharing" everything.

Because only male energy has the strength to rise up against oppression and fight for human rights, the suppression of male energy is key to keeping the population in a state of eternal acquiescence.

Stated Goal #6: Ensure availability and sustainable management of water and sanitation for all.

Hidden Reality: Allow powerful corporations to seize control of the world's water supplies and charge monopoly prices to "build a new water delivery infrastructure" that "ensures availability."

Stated Goal #7: Ensure access to affordable, reliable, sustainable, and modern energy for all.

Hidden Reality: Penalize coal, gas, and oil while pushing doomed-to-fail "green" energy subsidies to brain-dead startups headed by friends of the White House who all go bankrupt in five years or less.

The green startups make for impressive speeches and media coverage, but because these companies are led by corrupt idiots rather than capable entrepreneurs, they always go broke (and the media hopes you don't remember all the fanfare surrounding their original launch).

Stated Goal #8: Promote sustained, inclusive, and sustainable economic growth, full and productive employment, and decent work for all.

Hidden Reality: Regulate small businesses out of existence with government-mandated minimum wages that bankrupt entire sectors of the economy. Force employers to meet hiring quotas of LGBT workers while mandating wage tiers under a centrally planned work economy dictated by the government. Destroy free market economics and deny permits and licenses to those companies that don't obey government dictates.

Stated Goal #9: Build resilient infrastructure, promote inclusive and sustainable industrialization, and foster innovation.

Hidden Reality: Put nations into extreme debt with the World Bank spending debt money to hire corrupt American corporations to build large-scale infrastructure projects that trap developing nations in an endless spiral of debt.

See the book *Confessions of an Economic Hit Man*[3] by John Perkins to understand the details of how this scheme has been repeated

---

3 https://en.wikipedia.org/wiki/Confessions_of_an_Economic_Hit_Man

countless times over the last several decades.

Stated Goal #10: Reduce inequality within and among countries.

Hidden Reality: Punish the rich, the entrepreneurs, and the innovators, confiscating nearly all gains by those who choose to work and excel. Redistribute the confiscated wealth to the masses of non-working human parasites that feed off a productive economy while contributing nothing to it...all while screaming about "equality!"

Stated Goal #11: Make cities and human settlements inclusive, safe, resilient, and sustainable.

Hidden Reality: Ban all gun ownership by private citizens, concentrating guns into the hands of obedient government enforcers who rule over an unarmed, enslaved class of impoverished workers. Criminalize living in most rural areas by instituting *Hunger Games*-style "protected areas" that the government will claim are owned by "the People," even though no people are allowed to live there. Force all humans into densely packed, tightly controlled cities where they are under twenty-four-hour surveillance and subject to easy manipulation by government.

Stated Goal #12: Ensure sustainable consumption and production patterns.

Hidden Reality: Begin levying punitive taxes on the consumption of fossil fuels and electricity, forcing people to live under conditions of worsening standards of living that increasingly resemble third world conditions. Use social influence campaigns in TV, movies, and social media to shame people who use gasoline, water, or electricity, establishing a social construct of nannies and tattlers who rat out their neighbors in exchange for food credit rewards.

Stated Goal #13: Take urgent action to combat climate change and its impacts.

Hidden Reality: Set energy consumption quotas on each human being and start punishing or even criminalizing *"lifestyle decisions"* that exceed energy usage limits set by governments. Institute total surveillance of individuals in order to track and calculate their energy consumption. Penalize private vehicle ownership and force the masses onto public transit, where TSA grunts and facial recognition cameras can monitor and record the movement of every person in society – like a scene ripped right out of the film *Minority Report*.[4]

Stated Goal #14: Conserve and sustainably use the oceans, seas, and marine resources for sustainable development.

Hidden Reality: Ban most ocean fishing, plunging the food supply into an extreme shortage and causing a runaway food price inflation that puts even more people into economic desperation.

Criminalize the operation of private fishing vessels and place all ocean fishing operations under the control of government central planning. Only allow favored corporations to conduct ocean fishing operations (and make this decision based entirely on which corporations give the most campaign contributions to corrupt lawmakers).

Stated Goal #15: Protect, restore, and promote sustainable use of terrestrial ecosystems, sustainably manage forests, combat desertification, and halt and reverse land degradation and halt biodiversity loss.

Hidden Reality: Roll out Agenda 21 and force humans off the land and into controlled cities. Criminalize private land ownership, including ranches and agricultural tracts. Tightly control all agriculture through a corporate-corrupted government bureaucracy whose policies are determined almost entirely by Monsanto while being rubber-stamped by the USDA. Ban woodstoves, rainwater collection, and home gardening in order to criminalize self-reliance and force total dependence on government.

Stated Goal #16: Promote peaceful and inclusive societies for sustain-

---

4   Minority Report, http://www.imdb.com/title/tt0181689/

able development, provide access to justice for all, and build effective, accountable, and inclusive institutions at all levels.

Hidden Reality: Grant legal immunity to illegal aliens and "protected" minority groups, who will be free to engage in any illegal activity, including openly calling for the mass murder of police officers because they are the new protected class in society. "Inclusive institutions" means granting favorable tax structures and government grants to corporations that hire LGBT workers or whatever groups are currently in favor with the central planners in government. Use the IRS and other federal agencies to selectively punish unfavorable groups with punitive audits and regulatory harassment, all while ignoring the criminal activities of favored corporations that are friends of the political elite.

Stated Goal #17: Strengthen the means of implementation and revitalize the global partnership for sustainable development.

Hidden Reality: Enact global trade mandates that override national laws while granting unrestricted imperial powers to companies like Monsanto, Dow Chemical, RJ Reynolds, Coca-Cola, and Merck. Pass global trade pacts that bypass a nation's lawmakers and override intellectual property laws to make sure the world's most powerful corporations maintain total monopolies over drugs, seeds, chemicals, and technology. Nullify national laws and demand total global obedience to trade agreements authored by powerful corporations and rubberstamped by the UN.

Total Enslavement of the Planet by 2030

As the UN document says, "We commit ourselves to working tirelessly for the full implementation of this Agenda by 2030." If you read the full document and can read beyond the fluffery and public relations phrases, you'll quickly realize that this UN agenda is going to be forced upon all the citizens of the world through the invocation of government coercion.

Nowhere does this document state that the rights of the individual will be protected, nor does it even acknowledge the existence of human rights granted to individuals by the Creator. Even the so-called "Universal Declaration of Human Rights" utterly denies individuals the right to self-defense, the right to medical choice, and the right to parental control over their own children. [End of Michael Snyder quote] [End of MIA October 2015 segment]

Conclusion

We must know who the real enemy is and label them. Many of the agenda items described above are already in various stages of implementation by the socialist governments of America and Europe (including Canada, Australia, and other western New World Order governments). Do you see where all of this is going? The UN is planning nothing less than global government tyranny that enslaves all of humanity, while calling the scheme "sustainable development" and "equality."

George Orwell's *1984*[5] has finally arrived and it's all being rolled out under the fraudulent label of "progress." And, of course, it was fully supported over the Bush years and the Marxist Obama regime and the global/socialist controllers behind it (and, of course, Hillary is a strong supporter as well). The globalists have even enlisted the Pope to help push the agenda. This Pope is a NWO plant.

And now you may have a better understanding of exactly what President Donald J. Trump is up against. I will cover this just a bit more in another chapter in this book. Right now we will explore how to make sense of this madness and how to detect truth from lies in this controlled matrix in which we live.

---

5 1984, https://en.wikipedia.org/wiki/Nineteen_Eighty-Four

CHAPTER EIGHT: THE ENEMIES OF DONALD TRUMP

DONALD TRUMP IS UNDER AN UNPRECEDENTED, relentless assault from every which way to Sunday and this will not let up. He will receive faulty intelligence. He will be tripped up every way possible. He is being sabotaged from within. An illegal coup d etat. I will cover this extensively in my next book, along with an in depth discussion of the Deep State. Again, we must know who our enemy is. So, who are the enemies of Donald Trump?

Enemies of Donald Trump

You know much about a person by their friends. You know a lot about a person by their enemies. The enemies of Donald Trump are no friends of mine, and are no friends of capitalism, individual freedoms, or sovereign nations. So, who are the enemies of Donald Trump and just what is Trump up against?

It is not just the U.S. House and Senate that he has to overcome; it runs much deeper than this. Trump is up against the tyrannical ruling elite and its once secret agenda for global domination via the New World Order. You should know the enemies of Donald Trump, with names such as the Rothschilds, George Soros, the Rockefellers,[1] the Bush crime family, and the corrupt Clintons, to name but a few. This includes organizations such as the Bilderberg Group,[2] CFR, Tri-lateral commission, Skull and Bones,[3] the government media complex, Bohemian Grove[4] and so on, with treaties, policies, and agendas such as North American Union,[5] TPP, UN's Agenda 21 and UN's Agenda 2030 and so on. Don't believe me? Read Idea Scale's article "David Rockefeller's book *Memoirs* admits secretly conspiring for a NWO."[6]

We have psychopaths playing God.[7] These psychopaths[8] presently own, run and control every aspect of our lives with a very specific stated agenda to seize control over our lives, the resources on this planet, and the planet itself, while reducing the population to a stated amount of approximately 500 million people. Conspiracy theory? No – conspiracy fact. And this is why there is a never-ending, always increasing firestorm of assaults, attacks, traps, lies, and insidious people and programs being unleashed upon Donald J. Trump. We are at a crossroads for humanity, make no mistake about it.

You've heard the expression "It's the economy, stupid"? Who are the enemies of Donald Trump? The answer is "It's the New World Order, stupid." People like George Soros and the groups he funds, such as moveon.org and black lives matter, ISIS, Islamic terrorists, criminals, illegal aliens, warmongers, the political establishment

1 Nicholas Rockefeller admitted elite goal is 100% microchip population control, https://www.youtube.com/watch?v=oygBg6ETYIM
2 CLUB BILDERBERG: The TRUE Story of the BILDERBERG Group – ft. Daniel Estulin & Alex Jones, https://www.youtube.com/watch?v=lIPypdKHNA0
3 https://en.wikipedia.org/wiki/Skull_and_Bones
4 Bohemian Grove – Alex Jones, https://www.youtube.com/watch?v=FpKdSvwYsrE
5 NORTH AMERICAN UNION EXPOSED on Lou Dobbs w/ Marcy Kaptur & Bill Tucker, https://www.youtube.com/watch?v=Nsl7oQeGP08
6 http://opengov.ideascale.com/a/dtd/David-Rockefeller-s-book-Memoirs-admits-secretly-conspiring-for-a-NWO/4007-4049
7 https://johnmichaelchambers.com/bio-consciousness-creating-god-2045/
8 https://johnmichaelchambers.com/shadow-government/

(Democrats and Republicans), communists, socialists, fascists, racists (of many colors), left wing, radical, law-breaking lunatics and so on. These are some of the enemies of Donald Trump.

Then there are the blissfully ignorant who just don't get what is going on in the world around them and, of course, there are stupid people.

Friends of Trump

As a unifier, Trump's friends can be found on either side of the political fence – liberals, conservatives, democrats, republicans, independents, libertarians, people of many races and religions, the unemployed, both working class and the ultra-rich.

And honestly, at this stage of the game, all these categories are meaningless. People in favor of a nationalist for sovereignty vs. politics as usual can be considered friends of Trump – people who want to restore the Constitutional Republic and to protect and preserve the borders, language, and culture. Freedom-loving individuals who want to remain a sovereign nation and rebuild the country from every facet, top to bottom, inside and out. Trump's friends are those who realize that the American dream has become the American nightmare and perhaps the China, and NWO dream.

And so civilization is indeed at a crossroads. The human race and the universe itself are becoming more and more conscious of themselves and the tide is turning. After all, who would have ever expected this last election cycle and all that came with it? It was surreal. Donald Trump is President? Again, reminds me of *Back to the Future* where Doc says to Marty…

Doc: Then tell me, future boy, who's President of the United States in 1985?

Marty: Ronald Reagan.

Doc: Ronald Reagan? The actor? Then who's vice president? Jerry Lewis? I suppose Jane Wyman is the First Lady!

Marty: Whoa. Wait, Doc!

Doc: And Jack Benny is secretary of the treasury.

Marty: Doc, you gotta listen to me.

But yes, Donald Trump is President and this is no mistake. This is a good thing, as we are a culture and civilization in serious decline, a planet in peril. A full course correction is needed, and soon the masses will see this as so many already have. In this, there is hope.

You can't change people. They change themselves by their own decisions. You can influence them and guide them; meanwhile, the blissfully ignorant go along as though it were business as usual. It's not business as usual, and I can assure you of this.

We are indeed living in the age of an increasing number of smarter phones and an increasing number of dumbed-down people. Isaac Asimov once said, "The saddest aspect of life right now is that science gathers knowledge faster than society gathers wisdom." By and large, his quote is so true today.

Technology has advanced and continues to advance rapidly, and we have the technology today to solve many of the critical issues facing mankind and the planet, from air to water to food, and not just for some, but for all. For each and every one of us. You know we can put an end to starvation, so we must ask why we haven't. Children are starving to death every day and all we do is change the channel or surf another website.

The trouble is with the systems and institutions, such as central banks and the debt-based monetary and economic systems. Governments, international bankers, corporations, Hollywood, the medical industry "Big Pharma," secret societies, religions, and others are preventing forward progress in exchange for both profit and control and are again using a world of betrayal after trust while utilizing clever, deceptive techniques.

Time is short and change is now under way. At the time of this writing we are entering the next stage of what may be a prolonged period in human history that will make the dark ages look like a picnic in the park. So, we must stop and look at some of the *misconceptions* in our understanding of many aspects of life and living and then make the necessary *course corrections* so we can create and sustain our happiness.

SECTION III: MAKING SENSE OF THE MADNESS
Connecting the dots from lies to truths

CHAPTER NINE: THE MEDIA

MANY OF US HAVE BEEN AWARE of the media bias and corruption for decades, while others are just becoming aware of this and in no small part thanks to President Trump. News channels such as FOX, CNN, or MSNBC and the dying networks ABC, NBC, and CBS are nothing more than a media circus with a cast of circus characters reading their scripted talking points and following their marching orders in exchange for huge salaries and fame. They are purveyors of disinformation.[1]

JFK and The Media

The media are biased disinformation centers of negativity designed to further agendas and keep the populace entertained, frozen with fear, misinformed, and engaged in useless debates as they plow forward with their long-sought-after goals of controlling the masses via controlling the talking points of the day. The media circus that surrounds you is nothing but a smokescreen. Turn it off. Seek credible, non-biased resources.

President John F. Kennedy delivered a very important speech to the

---

[1] 43 Times Donald Trump Has Attacked The Media As A Presidential Candidate
http://www.huffingtonpost.com/entry/donald-trump-has-attacked-the-media-many
-many-times_56059e0de4b0af3706dc3cce

American Newspaper Publishers Association at the Waldorf Astoria in New York City on April 27, 1961 – a 19:43 must-listen-to speech.[2]

> *"The media is to inform and alert the American people. We expect you to point out our mistakes when we miss them. For without debate, without criticism, no administration and no country can succeed and no republic can survive."*

You see, we do need the media to question the authority of Washington, D.C. and to honestly and fairly report the findings to the American people. This, in the main, is not happening today to say the least.

> *"Our press is protected by the First Amendment, the only business in America specifically protected by the Constitution, not primarily to amuse and entertain, not to emphasize the trivial and the sentimental, not to simply give the public what it wants, but to inform, to arouse, to reflect, and to state our dangers and our opportunities, to indicate our crisis and our choices, to lead, mold, educate, and sometimes even anger public opinion."*

What a privilege it is for a for-profit business (media) to be protected by the First Amendment, and lo and behold they are violating the practices of true, valuable, and important reporting. Soon, with Trump in office, this will change. The media is in defense mode now.

> *"This means greater coverage and analysis of international news. Greater attention to improve greater understanding of the news and that government at all levels must meet its obligation to provide you with the fullest possible information outside the narrowest limits of national security. And so it is to the*

---

2 JFK Secret Societies Speech (full) "The President and the Press," https://www.youtube.com/watch?v=DznTND--4eI&t=25s

printing press, the recorder of man's deeds, the keeper of his conscience, the courier of his news that we look for strength and assistance, confident that with your help, man can be what he was born to be – free and independent."

– JFK

My, how far we have come.

More on the Media

We no longer have anything that even closely resembles a free and independent press whose job in part is to inform, reflect, and state our dangers and our opportunities.

Part of the responsibility of the press is in fact to openly and freely question policy from a President's administration, almost to the point of being a thorn in the side of the government. After all, the government is supposed to be working for and representing the people. Instead, we have a complete media circus.[3] A cast of highly paid mouthpieces and biased commentators. Nothing more than teleprompter readers of scripted agendas filled with deceit, lies, misinformation, and disinformation.

We talked about the Edison Research Group back in Chapter Two. Well, the major media outlets today are known as the "government media complex" (a term coined by Michael Savage[4] back in 1997), whose talking heads are nothing more than mouthpieces for the government and new world agenda. Today's media reeks of Orwell's *1984*[5] in a very big way.

Police are murdered almost daily in the U.S. today; the coverage is minimal and the White House is virtually silent. When blacks rape, murder, and burn a white woman,[6] the media is virtually silent. When

---

3 https://johnmichaelchambers.com/media-circus/

4 http://michaelsavage.com/

5 http://www.online-literature.com/orwell/1984/

6 https://johnmichaelchambers.com/racists-come-in-all-colors/

ISIS is raping, marrying, selling, enslaving, and killing young girls by the thousands, the media and the feminists are both silent. When ISIS rounds up hundreds of Christian children and guns them all down, you don't hear it much or see it on the news. ISIS has murdered and thrown men off buildings to their death simply because they are gay, yet you don't hear a word from the LGBT crowd and the media is virtually silent. I can go on and on. So please tune into independent sources and voices. Become a truth seeker, then a truth speaker. Boycott the fake media. It's long overdue.

A Nation Led By Lies, Dies

So where was the media[7] and the vetting process in 2008? Very busy, as I recall, deflecting our attention to the subject of the first black president, the deliberate, long-planned collapse of the global financial system, the existing disastrous presidency of Bush II, and the freak show surrounding Sarah Palin, rather than doing its job of true independent journalism, vetting and reporting on Barack Hussein Obama. And so look what happened in the past eight years. The media has, over time, destroyed this nation, and almost everyone agrees about this media circus,[8] yet few still think on their own.

The orchestrated attacks by the collective government media complex unleashed what is just the beginning of a firestorm of assaults against then candidate, then President Elect, and now President Trump. Why? Trump has singlehandedly upset the apple cart of the New World Order and all that this entails. End of story, period. Journalism is dead[9] in America and has been for a very long time. So, over time and right before our very eyes, a nation led by lies, dies.

---

7 https://johnmichaelchambers.com/where-was-the-media-in-2008-2/
8 https://johnmichaelchambers.com/media-circus/
9 JFK Secret societies speech, https://www.youtube.com/watch?v=97n-uqJC2Jw

Dylan Ratigan

Once in a great while you will find a voice of reason. A brave, common-sense commentator who diverges from the scripted agenda and actually says what he thinks on national television. This is one of those people, Dylan Ratigan. Turns out, of course, he was correct. Now the proverbial can that he mentioned has been kicked down the road, and that road has arrived.[10] Watch this short video (https://www.youtube.com/watch?v=gIcqb9hHQ3E) and I think you will agree. The debt that Dylan Ratigan speaks of is unsustainable and the piper will need to be paid and that time has now come.

The storm clouds are gathering[11] and it is only a matter of time before the great collapse occurs as part of the global shift of power and the financial reset that is at our doorstep. Heed the call.[12]

The MSM (mainstream media) can be described as The Devil's Radio. Many of us have been aware of the deceitful, bought and paid for, controlled government media complex for many years, while others (thanks to Donald Trump's brave and fierce stance against the media) are waking up to this reality.

Trump – "I'm Running Against the Media"

In a speech[13] given by Donald Trump on August 13, 2016 in Fairfield, Connecticut, Trump said, "I'm not running against crooked Hillary. I'm running against the media." Much of this speech was aimed at the media as well as at crooked, lyin' Hillary.

Perception is reality. The media has portrayed Trump as a racist, con man, bigot, womanizer, baby abuser, and so on, even comparing him to Hitler. His statements (okay, a bit over the top on occasion) have, for the most part, been completely blown out of proportion,

---

10 http://usadebtclock.com/
11 https://johnmichaelchambers.com/storm-clouds-are-gathering/
12 https://johnmichaelchambers.com/category/financial-economic/
13 Fantastic Anti Hillary Clinton Speech By Donald Trump At Rally in Fairfield, Connecticut 8/13/16 HD, https://www.youtube.com/watch?v=G_B9cgKpmtQ

taken out of context, twisted, perverted, and turned into complete lies. I challenge anyone to bring forth factual evidence of such charges the media and its mindless regurgitators have made against Donald Trump. They won't, because they can't. The truth is Trump has played them like a fiddle, gaining perhaps billions of dollars in media coverage for free. Trump, having been relentlessly hit hard by a corrupt media, counter punches while busting up and exposing this government media complex for what it is as their newspapers fail and cable network ratings plummet. Watch now for big changes in 2017 and beyond. Thank you, President Trump, for your bravery.

Democracy Matters: A Strategic Plan for America. This is a blueprint. It is also sub-titled "Media Matters for America". This document titled "Democracy Matters: A Strategic Plan for America" lays out specifically what their agenda is to render Trump ineffective and ultimately removed from office. Media Matters for America – Media Matters Fighting to Destroy Trump, is a well- funded, well organized blueprint which is being implemented on a daily basis on multiple fronts disrupting every move that is made by President Trump and has already proven to be causing delays, chaos and divisions in America. Read excerpts from this evil document below. This once "confidential" 49-page document by David Brock spells it out.

Media Matters Fighting to Destroy Trump

This 49-page document spells out their battle plan. This well thought out plan of attack begins in its opening sections titled "We Will Fight Everyday". It goes on to say…"We are going to fight for things in which we believe, and we are going to fight against any attempt to erode the cornerstone work and values of the progressive movement and this pluralistic nation." The document continues its assault against President Trump and this movement by saying "We are going to resist the normalization of Donald Trump, his every conflict of interest, his every bit of cronyism, his every move towards authoritarianism, his every subversion of our democratic systems and principles, his every radical departure from foreign and domestic policy norms." They conclude their opening statement by saying "We are going to contest every effort, at every level of government, to limit rights, rescind protections, entrench inequality, redistribute wealth upwards, or in any other way fundamentally undermine the tenets of egalitarianism that must serve as the bedrock for our democracy."

"We will fight every day. We are going to fight for the things which we believe, and we are going to fight against any attempts to erode the cornerstone work and values of the progressive movement and this pluralistic nation. We are going to resist the normalization of Donald Trump. His every conflict of interest, his every bit of cronyism, his every move towards authoritarianism, his every subversion of our democratic systems and principles, his every radical departure from foreign and domestic policy norms." This is an excerpt from the document produced by Media Matters marked "Private and Confidential" titled "Democracy Matters: A Strategic Plan for America".

Under a program called CREW in the once confidential and private "Media Matters for America" 49-page document, states in part the following, "Trump will be afflicted by a steady flow of damaging information, new revelations, and an inability to avoid conflicts issues. The Trump administration will be forced to defend illegal conduct in court. Powerful industries and interest groups will see their power begin to wane. Dark money will be a political liability in key states". De-legitimizing Trump is becoming popular among those who do not support Trump and this de-legitimization is widespread but perhaps Trump will rise above and prevail over time. The battle has begun.

De-legitimizing Trump

This scathing report also covers a program called Shareblue and lays out just how they intend to de-legitimize Trump via social media. The document states in part "Shareblue will take back social media for the Democrats. We will delegitimize Trump's presidency by emboldening the opposition and empowering the majority of Americans who oppose him. Shareblue will be the dynamic nucleus of a multi-platform media company that informs, engages and arms Americans to fight. Here's what success looks like:

1. Shareblue will become the de-facto news outlet for opposition leaders and the grassroots.
2. Trump allies will be forced to step down or change course due to news published by Shareblue.
3. Under pressure from Shareblue, Democrats will take more aggressive positions against Trump.
4. Shareblue will achieve financial sustainability while diversifying content offerings and platforms.
5. Top editorial writing talent will leave competitors to join Shareblue."

The document goes on to say "Right now our institutions are among the critical few that stand between the America we love and the abyss. We must protect and defend our Democratic values. We will not back down. We will only move forward."

Conclusion

Fake News is now branded across the globe. Thank you President Trump. In my next book I will take this subject on in greater detail as there is a strong possibility that many in the Fake News media will be held accountable too. You see there are things called laws. 18 US

Code Sec. 2384 & 2385 which addresses seditious conspiracy and advocating the overthrow of a government.

"In a time of universal deceit, telling the truth is a revolutionary act."

— *George Orwell, 1984*

CHAPTER TEN: HEGELIAN DIALECTIC

THE HEGELIAN DIALECTIC[1] IS THE BLUEPRINT for directing our thoughts and actions into conflicts that then lead us to a predetermined solution. Plays right into divide and conquer. We must come to understand how the Hegelian dialectic forms our perceptions of this world, and if we don't come to understand this, then we will not realize that we are actually helping to implement the vision.[2] When we remain unknowingly locked into dialectical thinking, we cannot see out of that controlled matrix.

In 1847, Karl Marx and Friedrich Engels used Hegel's theory of the dialectic[3] to support their economic theory of communism. Today, Hegelian-Marxist[4] thinking permeates our way of life and our social and political structure. It is imperative that we break this and step outside the dialectic. This is how we begin to return to our own thoughts

1 http://www.marxists.org/reference/archive/hegel/works/ol/encycind.htm

2 Small Groups and the Dialectic Process, http://www.crossroad.to/articles2/04/3-purpose. htm#vision

3 http://web.archive.org/web/20080128195659/http:/www.calvertonschool.org/waldspurger/pages/ hegelian_dialectic.htm
20terror&oq=governm%20ent%20admits%20false&aqs=chrome.3.69i57j0l3.17409j0j7

4 What is the Hegelian Dialectic? http://www.crossroad.to/articles2/05/dialectic.htm

and conclusions and releases us from controlled and guided thought. Tell everyone you know about the Hegelian dialectic to help awaken the masses.

Divide and Conquer

Most information disseminated by the media machine and all its accomplices, such as Hollywood, for example, is nothing more than predictive programming and is false and misleading. This leads, of course, to division amongst the people, which plays right into their hands, divide and conquer.

With the divide-and-conquer strategy, we have the man behind the curtain winning as he gets his perceived opponents to fight amongst themselves. This is a way of keeping those in a position of power in power by making the people disagree with each other so that they are unable to join together and remove those from their position of power. Think this through. The people simply regurgitate the spoon-fed talking points from the news like a well-programmed robot.

And since they run the media machine, the education system, and much more, you can see how powerful and how effective they are. Thus, a divisive world in chaos and crisis.

We must avoid falling for the Hegelian dialectic and become skillful at recognizing when it is employed. This becomes as easy as breathing once you really see it and get it. Anytime a major problem or issue arises in society, think about who will gain or profit from it. Turn off the mainstream news or at least completely disregard what the machine is saying so that you can remove yourself from the situation. Take a step back to look at it from a third-party perspective. See the so-called "problem," look at who is reacting, why and in what way. Then look for who is offering up the "solution" and carefully watch the media's agenda.

This may be one of the most important things to fully understand in this section, "Making Sense of the Madness." It would be well worth your time to look at some of the links that have been provided and continue your research.

Once you get this, all things begin to fall into place. We must all come to understand the Hegelian dialectic, and once we do, we will see many of the events unfolding in a very different light, and then there is no turning back. To summarize this in the simplest way: Problem – Reaction – Solution.[5]

Problem-Reaction-Solution

A large-scale problem is created anticipating the reaction of the masses. The people then demand a solution, and the solution is not a solution but rather what the creators of the problem desired (but could not easily get implemented without the large-scale problem).

And so the problem is created and the people now willingly accept the "solution": war, wiretapping, privacy intrusions, gun confiscation – whatever serves the interest of these psychotic perpetrators and merchants of chaos.

Another example of this could be the school shootings since Columbine in Colorado back in the 1990s to the present day. This illustrates problem-reaction-solution. Problem: dead children from guns in school. Reaction: outrage over safety for children. Solution: ban guns, "please take away our right to bear arms."

I can cite all kinds of examples of the implementation of the Hegelian dialectic being used around the world today. These are what are known as "False Flag Operations."[6] This, too, is an important subject as false flag operations occur on a daily basis all over the world to an unsuspecting ignorant populace.

---

5 David Icke – Problem Reaction Solution – Hegelian Dialectic and Terrorism, https://www.youtube.com/watch?v=nad6lTWCHFo
6 https://www.google.com/search?sourceid=chrome-%20psyapi2&ion=1&espv=2&ie=UTF-%208&q=gov.%20admits%20to%20false%20flag%

CHAPTER ELEVEN: FALSE FLAGS

THE REALITY OF THIS WORLD – now that's a conspiracy. False flag operations[1] have been employed by governments all over the world, and this has been going on for decades. Important questions to ask are: A) Who had the most to gain? B) Who had the motive? C) Who had the most to lose? False flag operations are clandestinely launched to stir the emotions of the people to the point of either fear or anger – so much so that they will accept some government solution that otherwise would not have been accepted by the masses.

For example, there is of course the assassinations of JFK, RFK, and MLK, and the attacks of September 11, 2001,[2] which brought us the NSA phone taps, the Patriot Act, NDAA, and much more. Then there was the Boston Marathon Bomber, where armed police shut down the city of Boston and enacted essentially martial law, with unannounced private home invasions with military gear and without warrants. And of course there are scores of senseless killings in the American schools

---

1 53 ADMITTED False Flag Attacks, http://www.washingtonsblog.com/2015/02/x-admitted-false-flag-attacks.html
2 HOW DID WORLD TRADE CENTER 7 FALL? https://www.youtube.com/watch?v=8T2_nedORjw

since Columbine in Colorado as an attempt to control firearms with the ultimate goal of eliminating the Second Amendment rights of American citizens.

These few examples of false flag operations are very much in line with the Hegelian dialectic,[3] problem-reaction-solution,[4] with the solution often being a loss of liberty in some fashion or another and mass public support of some government action.

Surveys show that most people no longer trust the mainstream media and not without reason; therefore, it is wise to study false flag operations and the Hegelian dialectic and become skillful at identifying when these false flags do indeed occur. This is not a time for ignorance. Governments around the world admit to the implementation of false flag ops.

False Flags a Conspiracy Theorist Fantasy? – Not!

False flag terrorism is defined as a government attacking its own people, then blaming others in order to justify acting or going to war against the people it blames. Can you say war with Iraq? Wikipedia defines it: "False flag operations are covert operations conducted by governments, corporations, or other organizations, which are designed to deceive in such a way that they appear as if they are being carried out by other entities, groups, or nations than those who actually planned or executed them." Weapons of mass destruction?

False flag operations are clandestinely launched to stir the emotions of the people to the point of either fear or anger, bringing the populace into conflict, so much so that they will accept some government solution that otherwise would not have been accepted by the masses.

The following historical research can be found in the McAlvany Intelligence Advisor,[5] December 2015 issue.

3   http://en.wikipedia.org/wiki/Dialectic#Hegelian_dialectic
4   David Icke – Problem-Reaction-Solution Explained, https://www.youtube.com/watch?v=Xdkh1xaZHts
5   https://mcalvanyintelligenceadvisor.com/subscribe-today

Japan

Japanese troops set off a small explosion on a train track in 1931 and falsely blamed it on China in order to justify an invasion of Manchuria.

Germany

Nazi General Franz Halder also testified at the Nuremberg trials that Nazi leader Hermann Goering admitted to setting fire to the German parliament building in 1933, and then falsely blaming the communists for the arson. The Reichstag fire was the excuse for a state of emergency, martial law, and the triggering of a total dictatorship in the Nazi Third Reich, all within twenty-four hours of the classic false flag attack.

Russia

Soviet leader Nikita Khrushchev admitted in writing that the Soviet Union's Red Army shelled the Russian village of Manila in 1939 while blaming the attack on Finland as a basis for launching the "Winter War" against Finland. Russian President Boris Yeltsin agreed that Russia had been the aggressor in the Winter War, and Putin acknowledged the same.

Turkey

The Turkish prime minister admitted that the Turkish government carried out the 1955 bombing on a Turkish consulate in Greece, also damaging the nearby birthplace of the founder of modern Turkey, and blamed it on Greece, for the purpose of inciting and justifying anti-Greek violence.

Britain

The British prime minister admitted to his defense secretary that he and American President Dwight Eisenhower approved a plan in 1957 to carry out attacks in Syria and blame it on the Syrian government as a way to effect regime change.

United States

The CIA admits that it hired Iranians in the 1950s to pose as communists and stage bombings in Iran in order to turn the country against its democratically elected prime minister. Then there is the Oklahoma City bombing, Columbine, the attacks of September 11, 2001, Sandy Hook, the Boston Marathon Bomber, San Bernardino, and many, many others as probable suspects for false flag ops.

Summary

Are false flags a conspiracy theorist's fantasy or a proven fact as history has indicated? In many cases, we can see that false flags are in fact covert operations, and we must come to recognize this and do our own due diligence. The media circus will never address this, as they follow their marching orders and remain complacent at best. In this increasingly dangerous world in which we live, it is time to move out of the fixed, spoon-fed ideas many of us have and face the facts. After all, facts are facts.

CHAPTER TWELVE: DETECTING TRUTH FROM LIES

NOW THAT WE HAVE SOME VERY IMPORTANT tools and resources, we can begin to see through this clever veil and smokescreen to recognize truth from lies. You will get so good at this, you'll know almost immediately, as False Flags typically follow the same sorts of patterns as described before in the Hegelian Dialectic, False Flags, and Problem-Reaction-Solution sections. You can use this as a tool to put an end to all useless arguments that we find ourselves engaging in. Stop them dead in their tracks simply by saying… "Wow, it's the Hegelian dialectic rearing its ugly face again." The person you are talking with will say, "What?" And you take it from there.

Once you know the truth, you must share the truth. Educate, direct, and inform others so they, too, will know. What a great way to assist our fellow man and our new commander in chief, wouldn't you say? If millions of us do this, we can make a difference. We must, as our time has come.

"We shall require a substantially new manner of thinking if mankind is to survive." – Albert Einstein

What we need is a breakthrough of awareness and an inner awakening of the truth of this world and of this universe that inspires us to make the necessary changes in our daily affairs and approach to life and living. This cannot, and will not, be accomplished without asking questions, without critical thinking, without getting out of our comfortable comfort zones (most often our self-controlled and self-afflicted traps), without trusting our instincts and innate intuitiveness, and without listening to our innermost cognitions, revelations, realizations, epiphanies, etc., and then making the necessary changes to effect positive outcomes. Yes, it's up to you. You and me. Look no further than the man/woman in the mirror. As a long-term optimist, I see this as a viable solution to the aforementioned short-term analysis. We must stop and take a look around to reassess ourselves, others, life, and the systems and structures that make this world go 'round. Do your due diligence. Seek truth – share truth with others. In my next book, I will delve into this subject in greater detail and will provide a list, an arsenal if you will, of alternative sites and sources for information here in the age of fake news.

"We now live in a nation where doctors destroy health, lawyers destroy justice, universities destroy knowledge, the press destroys information, religion destroys morals, and banks destroy the economy." – Chris Hedges

SECTION IV: RESURRECTING AMERICA

Leading America's Second Revolution

CHAPTER THIRTEEN: CIVILIZATION IS AT A CROSSROADS

WITH ALL THAT WAS ADDRESSED IN SECTION ONE, "The World in Which We Live," and in Section Two, "Making Sense of the Madness," we can easily see how and why it is that civilization is at a crossroads. We cannot, and we must not, become complacent and let down our guard or rest on the laurels of this most recent election. Why? Because the battle has just begun. Leading America's second revolution is laced with extreme dangers.

An event paralleling 911 or something significantly worse can be triggered overnight, be it a terror event or a market meltdown like we have never seen before. And challenging the Federal Reserve, NATO, NAFTA, the U.N., and the globalist agenda has its consequences, as we have seen from JFK to Gaddafi. Trump intends to challenge this in a very big way and has indicated a potential withdrawal from the

United Nations (let's hope so, and throw them out of the country while we're at it and then build a Trump Tower in its place!).

Do you think for one second that the ruling elite are just going to sit on the sidelines after decades and decades of work and allow all they have accomplished to simply be reversed without challenge? Do you think they suddenly have ridded themselves of the demonic claws that grip their souls? I shall say not. So much is at stake for them. After all, they own and control hundreds of trillions of dollars if not more, of which I am sure they do not want to lose control. And as you may recall from Chapter Three, "Shadow Government," in the section on psychopaths and sociopaths, these sick individuals are in a chronic state of fear. Now with President Trump in office, the scales are tipping and that fear is intensified. They know we know who they are and where they are. We are coming after them. It is they who are now on the run. Know this. They simply have no place to go; thus, the stage is set for the battle of battles. Do not buckle. Do not retreat. Stay the course. Trust the plan.

So, what can we expect in 2019 and beyond? Well, truth be told, only God knows, but if we are good students of history and if we understand the true world we are living in, this coupled with intelligent analysis, we can forecast some likely scenarios. One being they win and civilization rapidly declines into a global police state as indicated in U.N. Agenda 2030 with the NWO's long-stated goals of a one-world government, a one-world military, a one-world justice system, a one-world currency with complete control over every aspect of our lives, stripping away our God-given rights while reducing the population from approximately 7.4 billion people to about 500,000 million, coming to fruition. Or we will win. We will defeat these tyrannical globalists as Trump leads America's second revolution and we begin to heal the world as part of humanity's course correction. Think I am overstating this? Think again. This has just begun.

We have learned from the primaries of 2015 and 2016 that this is indeed a two-headed snake, a one-party system serving the same ruling master. True colors were revealed. Think of your "friends," family members, FB friends, associates, etc. True colors were revealed as in certain "newscasters," celebrities, the Bushes, the Clintons, Ted Cruz, John Kasich, and scores and scores of others on both sides of the aisle. Loyalty to a party is part of the trap. Don't fall for it. The battle we have now embarked upon is for "all the marbles." This is deadly serious, folks, no joke. No hyperbole, no sensationalism, no bias, this is not fear mongering, and nothing conspiratorial about it. The FEMA camps[1] (there are many) are waiting and are not very welcoming. Failure is not an option.

While, believe it or not, there are some, few, who say that Donald Trump is a ruling elite plant and puppet placed in office to carry out the NWO goals. I would disagree.

A Bumpy Beginning

As you may recall, we did see Donald in the early months of the campaign rallies continuously promote all his properties, deals, and pending deals. He had his wine and steaks on display as you may recall. Furthermore, he made numerous outrageous statements during the primaries that seemed self-destructive, for example saying he could kill someone and they would still vote for him. There were other gaffs and misrepresented, fluctuating stats he would report, like unemployment figures would range from 20 to 30% or more based upon who knows what. But then...

Filling stadiums and arenas day after day with record-breaking crowds, somewhere along the way Trump realized he could actually win. He saw there was a real movement taking place, of which he became the voice. He met with hundreds of evangelical leaders, pastors, etc., and the totality of this experience began to have an impact

---

1 Camp FEMA: American Lockdown (Documentary Conspiracy), https://www.youtube.com/watch?v=TqWLX6gQKWA

on him, a profound impact. Simply stated, he matured. He evolved and firmly decided to become President. He realized that he was a voice for the forgotten.

You can see from this point forward in his campaign rallies, he no longer promoted his products, properties, and companies. He refined his speech and toned down to an extent what some may consider to be outrageous statements. And this is where and when the attacks began to escalate against Trump as the left, the Clinton camp, and the ruling elite saw that he was not stepping aside. They did all they could, including the electoral process RNC shenanigans in Colorado for example. Many were coming out against Trump at that time leading up to the GOP nomination and even shortly thereafter, and mostly from within his own party. There was a long list of Trump defectors and non-supporters within the Republican party beyond Cruz, Bush, and Rubio. Even Reince Priebus and Paul Ryan were not supportive of Trump leading up to, and even shortly after the nomination. The wise ones among us were on to them from day one. Look now, they are gone.

Did Trump cut a deal and change horses midstream? Perhaps we shall never know. Some say he was groomed for this position for decades with the theory that the ruling elite are fighting among themselves; Trump will be used to accomplish certain issues and will be "protected" so long as he follows the agenda. Or maybe all these theories within these inner circles are hogwash. Maybe Trump went into this from day one wholeheartedly, with full intentions to run and win the presidency to make America great again. What we do know is that Donald J. Trump is the 45th President of the United States, and this is historical and unprecedented. With Trump in office, there is hope. Watch these videos on YouTube titled Q-Plan to Save the World. Q-We are the Plan and Q-From Dark to Light. It is my belief, you will find the truth in these videos. I will cover this to a great extent in my next book due out in the winter of 2020.

Remember the Hegelian dialectic, false flags and problem-reaction-solution? This will be employed on a daily basis over time, with the occasional horrific event here and there. How do I know this? Because it's been done before. It is being done right now, and the ruling elite establishment are shaking in their shorts, make no mistake. The stakes are quite high in dealing with these psychopaths. I am not a pessimist. I am a short-term realist and a long-term optimist.

I believe the decisions that we make right here, right now, will determine how we live out the rest of our lives and beyond. We must all decide, as we are all responsible. It's become a slogan to sell some corporate merchandise, but I think Gandhi intended these words for a much higher purpose when he said, "Be the change that you wish to see in the world." So naturally it's up to you, me, each and every one of us. We must begin with the man (woman) in the mirror. Civilization is at a crossroads. We have divine intervention on our side. We must heed the call and step up to the plate. It is simply and truly up to us. This one is for "all the marbles."

CHAPTER FOURTEEN: BATTLE BEGINS – BIG PHARMA

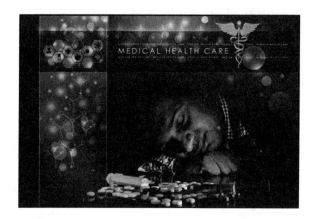

THE WORD "BATTLE" IS MOST APPLICABLE. Nearly (if not all) of Trump's policies will be met with great challenge and will not be overcome without a battle. Donald Trump's vision to "Make America Great Again" is diametrically opposed to the tyrannical globalist's view of America's place in this world. This chapter and the remaining chapters in this section will cover but some of the key challenges facing Trump, America, and the world in this battle to resurrect America through the second revolution. Share this with your liberal friends. If we overcome the issues and battles laid out in this section, we are well on our way to winning the ultimate battle and resurrecting America.

Big Pharma

I strongly urge you to read about the challenges facing the Trump administration and the people of this country when it comes to Big Pharma. Please visit this eye-opening tell-all series of posts on my blog site to become more familiar with what we are up against and to let this new administration know that we demand change. It is a nine-part series written by Dr. Richard Davis, MD, titled, "The Things Your Doctor Won't Tell You."[1] This is a must-read.

Vaccinations – Whose Decision Is It, Anyway?

Contributed by vaccine expert Sherri Tenpenny, DO

There has been much discussion about using schools for all-out vaccination campaigns for flu shots. Schools are becoming selected sites to become flu shot clinics; they have already been designated as gathering places during emergency events, such as tornadoes and hurricanes. Public health officials claim that schools are the most efficient ways to reach school-aged children and their parents. Some school-issued permission slips require parents to be present when their child is vaccinated if the child is in kindergarten through second. For older students, the presence of parents during vaccination is voluntary. The guidelines vary by state. If the government declares a pandemic flu emergency, will permissions be overlooked and will contraindications be taken into consideration?

Parental Consent vs. Physicians and the State

Parents have fewer rights over the health and welfare of their children than they may recognize. This concept reaches back into antiquity when the rulers in Sparta forcibly removed children from families so they could be indoctrinated with the willingness and importance of dying for the State in war.[2] This was also the model for Plato's idealized Republic. Interestingly, in 1918, the Congress of the Communist Party's education workers in Russia asserted, "We must remove the

---

1 https://johnmichaelchambers.com/the-things-your-doctor-wont-tell-you-part-1/
2 "The Free Market and Education, A Review," by Ken Schoolland. 1996. www.fff.org/aboutus/press/schooland.asp

children from the crude influence of their families."[3]

When it comes to medical decisions, physicians are charged with ensuring that the medical standard of care, defined as a treatment process that a clinician should follow for a given circumstance, is carried out on children, even over the objections of their parents. Doctors not only have the right to step in. All states have laws making it mandatory to report perceived medical abuse and neglect to Children's Protective Services (CPS). Physicians usually make the call when s/he feels the action – or inaction – of a parent places the child in danger of death or disability. A common example is a forced transfusion of blood to save the life of a child whose parents are Jehovah's Witnesses. However, not vaccinating has come under scrutiny and in some circles is viewed as medical neglect. The American Academy of Pediatrics recently concluded that "Continued (vaccine) refusal after adequate discussion should be respected unless the child is put at significant risk of serious harm (as, for example, might be the case during an epidemic). Only then should state agencies be involved to override parental discretion on the basis of medical neglect."[4]

Wide support and extensive court precedence exist to back a doctor's discretion to call in CPS. The rationale for this authority was clearly written in a 1996 paper that states, "Whether (the guardians) are sincere, sane, and in every other capacity model parents, their insistence upon treatment that is scientifically inferior to conventionally accepted treatment is abusive, even if their intent is not."[5] The current system, in its original intent, was set up to protect obviously abused and neglected children. The system would be a good one if medical professionals were amenable to common sense.

Unfortunately, common sense isn't very common these days,

---

3 Ibid. Ken Schoolland. www.fff.org/aboutus/press/schooland.asp

4 Salmon DA, Omer SB. "Individual freedoms versus collective responsibility: immunization decision-making in the face of occasionally competing values." Emerg Themes Epidemiol. September, 2006. 27; 3:13, http://www.ncbi.nlm.nih.gov/pubmed/17005041?dopt=AbstractPlus&holding=f1000,f1000m,isrctn

5 Rosen, J Emergency Med. 1996;14:241-243.

and disagreeing with your doctor can lead to serious consequences. Because the government agrees that "Doctor Knows Best," parents can be deemed unfit when they refuse a medical treatment. The CPS can remove children from the home until a judge determines proof of parental fitness. The judge can also be the doctor himself: Physicians have the right to eject entire families from their practice when an obstreperous patient refuses, or even questions, routine vaccinations.

Several high-profile standoffs have occurred in the last several years where judges, medical doctors, and the state have forced medical treatments on children against the objections of their parents.

» In January 2005, thirteen-year-old Katie Wernecke was diagnosed with Hodgkin's disease. When Katie's parents, Michele and Edward Wernecke, refused radiation treatment for their daughter, the Texas CPS intervened. Katie was placed in foster care for four months and her mother was arrested on charges of interfering with child custody.[6]

» In July 2006, the story of nine-month-old Riley Rogers made the news when he was diagnosed with a kidney problem that required emergency surgery. His mother disagreed and smuggled her son out of the hospital. Several days later, he was found and sent back to the hospital; the mother was charged with second-degree kidnapping and sent to jail. As it turned out, the surgery was not emergently needed after all.[7]

» Also in 2006, the story of Abraham Cherrix, a juvenile, resulted in a change in the law in Virginia. After enduring three months of ineffective treatments for Hodgkin's lymphoma, Abraham rejected his doctor's recommendation for a second round of chemotherapy. He chose to use more natural, non-toxic methods that included alternative medicine. A

---

6   "State-sponsored medical terrorism: Texas authorities arrest parents, kidnap their teenage daughter, and force her through chemotherapy against her will" by Alexis Black. Jan. 3, 2006. http://www.newstarget.com/016387.html

7   "Baby undergoes surgery despite mom's worries." by M. Alexander Otto. The News Tribune. July 2nd, 2006

judge ordered him back to chemotherapy, starting a debate on whether the government should get involved in family medical decisions. A compromise was reached in Accomack County Circuit Court: Abraham was not required to have chemotherapy if his family consented to treatment with a radiation oncologist who used both conventional and alternative methods. As a result of this high-profile case, Gov. Timothy M. Kaine signed a bill dubbed "Abraham's Law," giving parents and children more leeway in refusing medical treatment.[8]

These stories should raise the eyebrows of every parent, leading them to ask, "Who really owns your child?" and more to the point, "Who owns your child's *body*?" At what age does a child "officially" become the age of majority in the U.S. and have the right to decide what goes in his body?

Children Making Adult Decisions

The answer varies widely among the states, and in some locales, the very young have the right to make very big decisions. For example, a youth can legally get married with parental consent in Georgia, Mississippi, Michigan, and North Carolina when fifteen years of age. In Texas, fourteen-year-olds can wed with judicial consent, and amazingly, New Hampshire and Pennsylvania will even allow thirteen-year-old girls to marry with parental consent and court permission.[9]

However, most states seem to delineate sixteen years of age as the transition to adulthood. Nearly every state will allow sixteen-year-olds to marry with parental consent. At sixteen, a teen can hold a full-time job, travel alone outside the country, hold a driver's permit, and have full responsibility for someone's children as a babysitter. In many states, a sixteen-year-old can even be tried as an adult for murder.

8 "Assembly Gives 14-Year-Olds A Say on Key Medical Care," Washington Post. February 24, 2007.
9 http://en.wikipedia.org/wiki/Marriageable_age

When it comes to consent to medical care, the focal point of the debate over a minor's access to confidential services and the right to determine his or her own care originated in 1970 with the passage of the Title X family planning program. Since its inception, services supported by Title X have been available to anyone who needs them without regard to age.[10]

With the passage of time, the ability for minors to legally and fully consent to a range of sensitive health care services – including sexual and reproductive health care, mental health services, and alcohol and drug abuse treatment – has expanded dramatically. The trend was based on the presumption that while parental involvement in minors' health care decisions is desirable, many minors will not participate in medical services if forced to involve their parents. In most cases, state consent laws apply to all minors aged twelve and older. These examples are eye-popping:

» In twenty-five states and the District of Columbia, all minors (twelve and older) can receive contraceptive services without parental participation.

» In twenty-eight states and the District of Columbia, all minor parents have the right to place their child for adoption. Of these, only four states (LA, MI, MN, and RI) require parental consent.

» Three states (CT, ME, MD) and the District of Columbia explicitly allow minors, twelve years of age and older, to consent to an abortion without involvement or notification of a parent. Only twenty-two states require parental consent, and only eleven require a parent to be notified prior to an abortion.[11]

» Of the thirty-five states with specific statutes, thirty states

---

10 Minors and the Right to Consent to Health Care. The Guttmacher Report on Public Policy. August, 2009. http://www.guttmacher.org/pubs/tgr/03/4/gr030404.pdf

11 An Overview of Minors' Consent Laws. The Guttmacher Report. September 1, 2009. http://www.guttmacher.org/statecenter/spibs/spib_OMCL.pdf

allow a minor to obtain authorization for an abortion from a judge without informing her parents. This option, given to protect a minor's constitutional right to privacy, has been upheld by the U.S. Supreme Court.[12]

All this latitude has been given to minors to ensure they have rights for consenting to treatment but, and this is *key*, they have few or no rights when it comes to *refusing* medical treatment forced upon them by doctors and the government, even when their parents support their right to refuse.

So, where is the line between the right to refuse medical treatment, or a vaccine, and the right of the state to forcibly collide, especially in the event of a declared national emergency? Who gets to make the decision? Will it be parents and smart teens, or persons in white lab coats and black robes? For me, I will fight to maintain the line between me and "them" at the level of my skin. [End of Dr. Tenpenny section]

---

12 Ibid. Minors' Consent Laws

Chapter Fifteen: Battle Begins – The Economy

Connecting the Dots on the True State of the Economy

DONALD TRUMP'S ECONOMIC POLICY SPEECH took place on June 28, 2016 in Monessen, Pennsylvania, at Alumisource. In this speech[1] he covered the importance of restoring manufacturing and jobs back to the United States, as well as creating fair trade practices in the global marketplace. Donald Trump's policies are geared toward Nationalism and Americanism. The globalist's agenda will continue to obliterate the middle class, bringing the U.S. into a deteriorating third world country by design as the wealth and opportunities are distributed to other parts of the world.

---

1 Full Speech: Donald Trump Delivers Economic Policy Speech in Monessen, PA (6-28-16), https://www.youtube.com/watch?v=Ru3Cpf_Wkco

Trump spoke about the negative impact that NAFTA[2] and WTO[3] have had on America, reminding us that these two global trade agreements were signed by Clinton. He also warned about the TPP[4] and stated, once ratified, it would be a deathblow for American manufacturing. Trump went on to say that with Trans-Pacific Partnership, or TPP, foreign interests would come before American interests and we would give up our economic leverage to an international commission. He laid out seven specific points, which are summarized here on how to restore economic independence to America.

» Withdrawal from the TPP.
» Appoint trade negotiators.
» Direct Secretary of Commerce to identify trade violations and to end the abuses.
» Renegotiate or withdraw from NAFTA.
» Label China a currency manipulator.
» Trade cases filed against China in both the U.S. and at the WTO.
» China must stop the theft of American trade secrets.

The United States leaders, from Papa Bush to Clinton, from Clinton to Baby Bush, from Baby Bush to Hussein Obama, have been, decade by decade, sold out into the ruling elites' globalization and the New World Order. Trump will now attempt to reverse this and bring America back to its founding roots as laid out in the U.S. Constitution, the Declaration of Independence, and the Bill of Rights, thus leading America's second revolution.

Let's now talk about China. Look what has happened since NAFTA and the WTO. Do you think this happened by accident? No, by design of course.

2 https://en.wikipedia.org/wiki/North_American_Free_Trade_Agreement
3 https://www.wto.org/
4 https://en.wikipedia.org/wiki/Trans-Pacific_Partnership

American Nightmare Becomes the China Dream

Every picture tells a story.

I travel a lot and have spent most of my time in Asia over the past five years. I have driven past this billboard (see above photo) on a major highway in Bangkok. I have also seen similar postings in other locations and at airports in Asia, including many HSBC banks in Hong Kong, China, and the Philippines.

We used to strive toward creating and living the American dream. Thanks to decades of policies moving America into a one-world system, the American dream is now the American nightmare and has become the China dream. Like Donald Trump has said, China has been taking advantage of us with trade, jobs, and currency manipulation for decades, and the Chinese are laughing at us. He is right.

For many years China has been buying and stockpiling gold and other natural resources. This is in addition to owning and investing in gold mines in multiple countries, as well as oil and other natural resources. The BRICS alliance is strong and China has been preparing to replace (one step at a time) the U.S. dollar as a world reserve currency. In fact, the IMF already approved the RMB to be another world reserve currency for international trade, effective October 2016, with SDR (special drawing rights) backing. This is the credibility that was needed for China to provide an extra layer of confidence in the global marketplace.

This means that China can call upon the IMF to access the SDR, which really is just a backing of the RMB currency, again providing another layer of confidence in the global marketplace. A simple way to explain this is… The IMF is to the RMB as the Federal Reserve is to the U.S. dollar. Meet the new boss – same as the old boss.

The difference is the U.S. dollar is on life support, and the U.S. has a debt that will soon reach $23 trillion, with no jobs and horrific trade deficits. We owe China more than a trillion dollars and we simply cannot pay them back. Soon, when all pieces are in place, China may help create the collapse of the U.S. dollar by not allowing the conversion of the gold-backed RMB to or from U.S. dollars. There are so many possible scenarios but, with Donald Trump and his team, there is now hope.

You see, in this global shift of power that was underway, the financial power centers and the gold exchanges may be moving from west to east, from weak hands to strong hands, from New York and London, to China and Singapore. Soon, nobody will want the backed-by-nothing U.S. dollar fiat currency and will begin to move towards the Chinese RMB. When the U.S. dollar collapses, we may see the Amero[5] emerge to level the playing field. With all of this, if you take a bird's-eye view both past and future, these are stepping stones towards a one-world digital currency system some years down the line. Believe me, this money game is the jugular in this fight for power. Trump will be met with serious opposition. Donald Trump knows that the dollar is overvalued. Be prepared for some painful change.

China Buys the Chicago Stock Exchange?

The Chicago Stock Exchange and the Chinese have reached an agreement, and the Chinese will now add the Chicago Stock Exchange to its ever-increasing ownership of U.S. assets; not to mention, as reported

---

5 Lou Dobbs reports on the emerging "North American Union". It's real, it's happening! https://www.youtube.com/watch?v=UW_NBLaO6Ew

by Donald Trump, the U.S. has an annual trade deficit in excess of $400 billion with China.

The following is an excerpt from the book I co-authored back in 2013 titled *Surviving Global Governance*,[6] along with Richard Davis, M.D. and Kirk Elliott, PhD. The figures were taken from the McAlvany Intelligence Advisor reports of 2012. Have a look at these stats and facts. They are both shocking and revealing.

China Guts the U.S.

The Chinese, as we know from history, are very calculating and very patient. They take their time to achieve their desired goals. When you total up all imports and exports of goods, China is now the number one trading country on the entire planet.

China now has the largest new car market in the world, and residing in Asia as I am, when I am in China, I see all kinds of Ferraris, Lamborghinis, Aston Martins, and many other exotic cars on the streets. China has more foreign currency reserves than any other country on the planet, and is the number one gold producer and importer in the world.

Over the past decade, the Chinese economy has grown a staggering seven times faster than the United States economy, but this shouldn't be too much of a surprise, as the United States has lost 32% of its manufacturing jobs since the year 2000. (Note: Trump pledges to bring these jobs and dollars back to the U.S.) Many of those jobs have shifted over to China, and now are even going to other low-cost producing countries such as Cambodia, Vietnam, as the global power shift continues. The United States has lost an average of 50,000 jobs per month since China joined the World Trade Organization, along with over 56,000 manufacturing facilities over the past eleven years.

According to the Economic Policy Institute, America is losing 500,000 jobs to China every year. China now produces twice as many

6 https://johnmichaelchambers.com/books/surviving-global-governance-3/

automobiles as the U.S. (it's no wonder they are making bilateral trade agreements with oil-producing nations to try to get their oil). China produces eleven times as much steel as the United States, and over 90% of the global supply of rare earth elements. Shockingly, China is the number one supplier of components that are critical to the operation of the U.S. Defense System.

The average household debt in the United States is 136% of U.S. household income. In China, the average household debt is only 17% of average household income, and China is beginning to buy large amounts of real estate in an attempt to reduce some of their U.S. dollar holdings and acquire real tangible wealth. In 2011, one out of every ten houses sold was sold to a Chinese individual. The Chinese are the second largest block of home buyers in the United States. This is staggering to consider, as these are not temporary layoffs.

These are structural changes in the economy, and those jobs will not be coming back to America anytime soon, or anytime at all. For that to happen, the standard of living in Asia will have to increase, the standard of living in America will decrease, and when it equalizes, jobs could potentially come back to the United States, but that will take decades. Ladies and gentlemen, the global shift of power is under way, with major triggering events yet to unfold. Trump has much to deal with if he is to level the playing field with China. Again, we must be prepared.

Retail Stores Closing at an Alarming Rate

And the BHO administration talked about economic recovery? This is the result of many years of policy and tax strategies in accordance with globalization.

Storm clouds are gathering, and it is somewhat reflected in the retail sector. See the list of store closings below. Just like the real rate of unemployment is not 5%, there is no economic recovery. This list was compiled by the McAlvany Intelligence Advisory Report, March 2016. All over America, retail stores are shutting down at a stunning pace.

» Walmart is closing 269 stores, including 154 inside the United States.

» K-Mart is closing down more than two dozen stores over the next several months.

» JCPenney will be permanently shutting down forty-seven more stores after closing a total of forty stores in 2015.

» Macy's has decided that it needs to shutter thirty-six stores and lay off approximately 2,500 employees.

» The Gap is in the process of closing 175 stores in North America.

» Aeropostale is in the process of closing eighty-four stores all across America.

» Finish Line has announced that 150 stores will be shutting down over the next few years.

» Sears has shut down about 600 stores over the past year or so, but sales at the stores that remain open continue to fall precipitously.

Ah yes, and the blissfully ignorant move along as though it were business as usual. I can assure you it is not business as usual.

Unemployment is not in the 5% range as reported, but rather closer to 25%. Although the markets remain at these lofty levels, this controlled house of cards will come tumbling down in due time, mark my words. The days of the U.S. dollar serving as the world's reserve currency is rapidly coming to an end unless something is done and quickly. The derivatives' exposure is in the quadrillions.

Recently, there was the first bond to be sold with a negative yield.[7] The Euro and the European Union are collapsing – then consider this:

---

7 Behold! The First Covered Bond to Be Sold With a Negative Yield, http://www.bloomberg.com/news/articles/2016-03-08/behold-the-first-covered-bond-to-be-sold-with-a-negative-yield

As of February 29, 2016, the official debt of the United States government is $19.1 trillion ($19,125,455,057,426). This amounts to:

 » $59,196 for every person living in the U.S.
 » $153,511 for every household in the U.S.
 » 105% of the U.S. gross domestic product.
 » 548% of annual federal revenues.

At the close of the 2015 fiscal year (September 30, 2015), the federal government had roughly:

 » $8.3 trillion ($8,279,000,000,000) in liabilities that are not accounted for in the publicly-held national debt, such as federal employee retirement benefits, accounts payable, and environmental/disposal liabilities.
 » $26.7 trillion ($26,661,000,000,000) in obligations for current Social Security participants above and beyond projected revenues from their payroll and benefit taxes, certain transfers from the general fund of the U.S. Treasury, and assets of the Social Security trust fund.
 » $28.5 trillion ($28,500,000,000,000) in obligations for current Medicare participants above and beyond projected revenues from their payroll taxes, benefit taxes, premium payments, and assets of the Medicare trust fund. For additional vital statistics, visit www.justfacts.com[8] and www. shadowstats.com.[9] [End of MIA report]

The Big Short

You may recall the movie starring Steve Carell, Ryan Gosling, Christian Bale, and Brad Pitt. If you have not seen this yet, it should be on your movie bucket list for sure. *The Big Short* is a 2015 biographical comedy-drama based on the financial crisis and collapse of 2007–2008, which was triggered (in part) by the housing market and

8 http://www.justfacts.com/nationaldebt.asp
9 http://www.shadowstats.com/

other Wall Street/banking scandals. Well, soon, the "Biggest Short" will arrive at the global doorstep.

Having had a previous career as an independent financial advisor and then consultant for nearly fifteen years, I found this film to be accurate and chilling. At the end of the movie, they summarize what Brad Pitt and Steve Carell's characters are doing today, and it is subtle but telling. Pitts' character lives on an orchard growing food. Carell's character invests everything in water. Food and water, hmm. To me, food and water tells you all you need to know about where this is heading when the economic tsunami and the mother of all meltdowns wreaks havoc on the global economy.

The issues that caused the meltdown of 2008 are immeasurably worse today, and when they are ready (just like last time), the Globalists henchmen will collapse it all. It will make 2008 look like nothing more than a passing drizzle.

So what to do? The wrong thing to do is nothing. Solutions for your personal prosperity are outlined in the final section of this book. The other wrong thing to do is to trust the system. It is a fraudulent, controlled system. The Federal Reserve must be eliminated, end the Fed.

The Real Unemployment Rate

Over the years, Presidents have reported unemployment figures based on the category that serves them best. This is typical political deception.

This one is very easy to clear up once one has the facts. You see, politicians on both sides of the aisle like to show positive statistics so that they can take credit for such good results, get re-elected, and stay in power. Most people have come to distrust politicians (and the media), so I thought I would take just a moment and provide some resources from economists, not politicians, regarding the real rate of unemployment. First a description of the classifications, then an important, easy-to-read summary.

The Classifications

U-1: This is the narrowest definition of unemployment, counting only those who are unemployed for fifteen weeks or longer.

U-2: A slightly wider definition, including those who would be counted as U-1, plus all of those who have lost their jobs involuntarily and those who have completed temporary jobs. A recent example of a temporary job would be someone who took a job as a census taker for the 2010 Census, knowing that once it was completed, their employment with the Census Bureau would be terminated.

U-3: This is considered the official unemployment rate by the Department of Labor and the one most often cited in the media. This rate includes all those who are unemployed and are seeking employment, as well as those classified as U-1 and U-2.

U-4: This rate is U-3 plus those workers who are considered "discouraged workers." In laymen's terms, these are individuals who are unemployed but not looking for employment only because they think there are no jobs available and to look would be in vain.

U-5: This rate is U-4 plus those workers who are marginally attached to the labor force. Essentially it includes people who are unemployed and not looking for work for any reason, market related or not.

U-6: This rate is U-5 plus all those who are working part-time due to the poor jobs market, but who want and are available to work full-time. An example would be a recent college graduate working part-time as a waiter to get by, but would like to work full-time in his or her chosen field.

John Williams, PhD, is sort of the economist's economist when it comes to reporting statistics. Many of the more well-known "celebrity economists," if you will, go to John Williams for their stats and then they reflect and forecast based on these stats. You too can learn more by viewing one important webpage from John Williams. "Alternate Employment Charts"[10] says it all in a current, one-page, simple format.

Instead of properly informing the unsuspecting public of such an important statistic as unemployment, politicians choose to hide the facts by keeping the public they were sworn into office to serve improperly informed. The system is setting people up. Keep them dumbed down, uninformed, and dependent upon government for food, money, health care, and shelter. Meanwhile, don't forget this… the tick-tock-tick-tock of the USA debt clock.[11] Thank goodness with President Trump, we have the best employment numbers in recorded history.

What's a Derivative, Mommy?

"A derivative, my dear, is an invention by greedy men and women to try to make lots of money for themselves while producing no real value for anyone."

"I don't think that will end too well, do you, Mommy?"

"No, it will have a very bad ending, my dear. You are so right because you have common sense."

The largest financial time bomb in history is ticking. Created by our friends on Wall Street, derivatives are now estimated at over $700 trillion, and some estimates put that figure as high as $1.5 quadrillion. The year 2008 has taught us that this is the biggest speculative financial bubble in world history, and the entire global financial system itself is now at risk.

Derivatives are the largest and most speculative schemes creating

---

10 http://www.shadowstats.com/alternate_data/unemployment-charts
11 http://usadebtclock.com/

hundreds of billions in profits into the big banks and brokerage firms. According to estimates published in the McAlvany Intelligence Advisor, October 2015, the total United States bank exposure to derivatives is over $280 trillion and rising quickly.

A more technical definition is that derivatives are securities with a price that is dependent upon or derived from one or more underlying assets; financial instruments whose value is based on the performance of underlying assets such as stocks, bonds currency exchange rates, and real estate. The main categories of derivatives are futures, options, and swaps. Derivatives are financial instruments whose value is derived from the value of an underlying asset (such as gold, wheat, or other commodities) or other financial instruments including bonds, or market benchmarks such as interest rates.

"Wow, that sounds so smart and impressive, Mommy."

Is it really?

"No, my dear, it's just complex gibberish to keep us ignorant as the greedy corporations, financial centers and governments create huge profits at the risk of collapsing it all upon everyone, including themselves."

Derivatives and the Coming Global Meltdown

There are five "too big to fail/jail" banks in America. These banks collectively have approximately $300 trillion in derivatives. This list compiled from the McAlvany Intelligence Advisor, December 2015, can be seen below:

JP Morgan Chase
Total Assets: $2,476,986,000,000 (about $2.5 trillion)
Total Exposure to Derivatives: $67,951,190,000,000 (more than $67 trillion)

Citibank
Total Assets: $1,894,736,000,000 (almost $1.9 trillion)

Total Exposure to Derivatives: $59,944,502,000,000 (nearly $60 trillion)

Goldman Sachs
Total Assets: $915,705,000,000 (less than $1 trillion)
Total Exposure to Derivatives: $54,564,516,000,000 (more than $54 trillion)

Bank of America
Total Assets: $2,152,533,000,000 (a bit more than $2.1 trillion)
Total Exposure to Derivatives: $54,457,605,000,000 (more than $54 trillion)

Morgan Stanley
Total Assets: $831,381,000,000 (less than $1 trillion)
Total Exposure to Derivatives: $44,946,153,000,000 (more than $44 trillion)

In 2008, we were told that the potentially catastrophic problem of the *"too big to fail"* banks would be brought under control but, instead, they have grown 37% since that last recession. Currently, these five largest banks account for 42% of all loans in the U.S., and the six largest banks control 67% of all banking assets.

And it isn't just U.S. banks that are engaged in this type of behavior. As Zero Hedge recently detailed, the German banking giant, Deutsche Bank, has more exposure to derivatives than any of the American banks listed above. Deutsche has a total derivative exposure that amounts to €55 trillion or just about $75 trillion. That's about a hundred times greater than the €522 billion in deposits the bank has.

It is also five times greater than the entire GDP of Europe and approximately equal to the GDP of the entire world. It is no secret in the financial world that Deutsche Bank is in serious trouble – right now! Will the present German refugee crisis and resultant political upheaval trigger big problems in the German banking sector? We shall see.

There are scores of other economic data, such as the inflated stock market, the interest rate, sensitive bond markets, the debt debacle, the credit bubble, currency, and trade data that supports the notion there is a global financial meltdown on the horizon. It's time to hedge against this by getting out of the system, now, not later!

Global War on Cash

War on cash? Why?[12] The war on cash is a war against privacy and for people control. The global war on cash is escalating rapidly. Moving to a cashless society (globally) will not happen overnight, but is in fact being implemented right now across the globe. There are all sorts of restrictions for cash transactions taking place for "security measures" of course as an effort to thwart criminals, terrorists, drug runners, money launderers, and tax evaders and so on. Controlling cash and moving towards a cashless society is part of the new world we are rapidly emerging into by the ruling elite and the new world agenda.

United States: In the United States, there are so many controls, steps, and laws in place.

Sweden: Last year, Stockholm's KTH Royal Institute of Technology released a report[13] stating that the country is on track to completely eliminate cash transactions in the foreseeable future.

According to the McAlvany Intelligence Advisor, May 2015 issue, in Swedish cities, cash is no longer acceptable on public buses; tickets must be purchased in advance or via a cell phone text message. Many small businesses refuse cash, and some bank facilities have completely stopped handling cash. Indeed, in some Swedish towns it is no longer possible to use cash in a bank at all.

---

12 Aaron Russo RFID Human Implant Chip, https://www.youtube.com/watch?v=LGcatieMvfk
13 Cashless future for Sweden? https://www.kth.se/en/aktuellt/nyheter/
    cashless-future-for-sweden-1.597792

Italy: Besides a recent run on the banks, back in 2012, Italy lowered the legal maximum on cash transactions from €2,500 to €1,000.

Canada: Canada, presently losing ground against the U.S. dollar, is also heading towards a cashless system[14] in a series of ongoing efforts.

France: As of September 2015, it is illegal for French citizens to make purchases exceeding 1,000 Euros in cash.[15]

Norway: The largest bank in Norway demands a ban on cash.[16] Bank executive Trod Bentestuen said, "There are so many dangers and disadvantages associated with cash, that we have concluded that it should be phased out."

Denmark: The Danish government is en route to a 0% cash society by 2030.[17]

Advocates of a cashless society say that it would provide greater security (i.e., less robberies) for the public ("It's for your protection," as the TSA continually reminds us). Anti-cash advocates point to another alleged advantage of electronic transactions: they leave a digital trail that can be readily followed by the state, so governments can track their citizens' financial transactions – a capability dictators like Hitler would have liked to have. As one anti-cash "expert" on underground economies instructs us, "If people use more cards, they are less involved in shadowy economy activities." In other words, secreting their hard-earned income in places where it cannot be plundered by the state.

The whole point of a cashless economy is to make even the most intimate economic affairs of private citizens transparent to the state

---

14 More Canadians Going Cashless Thanks To Apps, Credit And Debit Cards, http://www.huffington-post.ca/2015/12/25/cashless-apps-debit-credit_n_8876896.html

15 http://www.connexionfrance.com/1000-euro-cash-payment-limit-france-september-money-laundering-17068-view-article.html

16 Norway's largest bank calls for total end to cash, http://www.thelocal.no/20160122/norways-largest-bank-calls-for-complete-end-to-cash

17 Denmark Pushes Forward with Cashless Payments, http://paymentweek.com/2015-12-23-denmark-pushes-forward-with-cashless-payments-9215/

and its fiscal and monetary authorities, who themselves hate and fear transparency as night owls do sunlight. And then there are the benefits that accrue to the government-privileged banking system from the demise of cash. One Swedish small businessman noted the connection. While he gets charged five kronor (80¢) for every credit-card transaction, he is prevented by law from passing this on to his customers. In his words, "For them (the banks), this is a very good way to earn a lot of money. That's what it's all about. They make huge profits." [End of MIA Report]

Swiss Economist Marc Faber recently said, "Basically, we are moving into an Orwellian society where they can check everything and cash will be one of the means where you can go somewhere and buy something and nobody would really know about it. Now they want to abolish it."

Privacy and freedom sort of go hand in hand if you think about it. There has certainly been a reduction of personal freedoms and individual liberties across the world, namely in the United States, and so, cash allows privacy. This is not part of the agenda moving forward. There is a war on cash, and you will see this increase in due time.

The ECB wants to do away with the €500 bill and there is also discussion to eliminate the $100 bill. According to Zero Hedge, the $100 bill accounts for a whopping 78% of all physical U.S. currency in circulation.

There are presently numerous restrictions, rules, and laws concerning cash in the U.S. Expect to see a reduction of the size (i.e., $100 bill to cease) of new and already circulated notes; further restrictions as to how much can be withdrawn from banks; as well as a significant reduction of cash to be carried across international borders.

There is not only a war on your mind; there is a war on your cash. This is yet another reason to begin building a proper ratio of gold and silver[18] as an insurance policy against the war on cash.

18 https://johnmichaelchambers.com/why-gold-why-silver-why-now/

Step-by-step as part of the new world agenda laid out in the United Nations Agenda 2030[19] (and many other programs by other organized bodies), we can see a move towards a cashless society. Debit and credit cards, electronic funds transfers/payments, online banking, all very much common practice today. Is it possible that all will be controlled via national ID cards? Then perhaps a global ID card eventually ending with the "chip at birth injection"? Control us from sophisticated AI technology which they already have in place? This is coming soon unless we defeat these psychopaths as Trump leads the second American revolution.

Trump Forecasts a Massive Recession

As a matter of public record, Donald Trump has good instincts and is quite intuitive. Trump forecasted the tragic events of September 11, 2001 as described in his book, *The America We Deserve*. He also warned about terror in Brussels. I delved into these in more detail in a blog post titled "Trump Warns America Is in Danger."[20] And now, more recently in an interview with Bob Woodward and Robert Costa from the Washington Post,[21] Donald Trump forecast a massive recession. The President and team are working behind the scenes to redirect this dwindling spiral. The Global Financial Reset has begun.

The Inevitable Market Crash

This section introduces tools and resources to not only survive, but to thrive through this second American revolution. It will also provide content for those who may be politically active. But first, we must address, with some detail, the inevitable market crash, as this is coming and this will affect all of us.

19 https://johnmichaelchambers.com/global-service-announcement-agenda-2030-part-i/
20 https://johnmichaelchambers.com/trump-warns-america-is-in-danger/
21 In a revealing interview, Trump predicts a 'massive recession' but intends to eliminate the national debt in 8 years, https://www.washingtonpost.com/politics/in-turmoil-or-triumph-donald-trump-stands-alone/2016/04/02/8c0619b6-f8d6-11e5-a3ce-f06b5ba21f33_story.html?wpisrc=al_alert-COMBO-exclusive%252Bnational

Some say the market will soar now that Donald Trump has been elected. Perhaps yes for a period of time. Some say the DOW, for example, may be on its way to 30,000, and higher (perhaps, unlikely though). I think there is more of a likelihood that the markets will collapse. It's not a matter of *if*, but rather *when* and *how*. Will it be an overnight, systemic collapse as in the financial crisis of 2008? Will it happen slowly but surely, this time perhaps one segment at a time? For example, bonds? Derivatives? Banking? Stocks? Real estate? Currency?

Will the ruling elite shadow government use this as a means to try to take down President Donald Trump? An attempt to discredit Trump and have the people and the world for that matter assign cause and blame to him, thus the people and government turning against him, leading to impeachment proceedings?

Perhaps the Bilderberg Group[22] and others will orchestrate the market collapse in some form or another, then blaming it on Trump only to be fueled by the government media complex bias machine. Remember, all recessions and depressions are now to a greater or lesser extent engineered and implemented by design. Donald Trump forecasted the tragic events of September 11, 2001 as described in his book titled "The America We Deserve". He also warned about terror in Brussels and then, in 2016, in an interview with Bob Woodward and Robert Costa from the Washington Post, Donald Trump forecasted a very massive recession. This day may be coming soon and without notice. Be prepared.

The Mother of all Meltdowns

The fact of the matter is the system is in a far worse condition than it was leading up to the collapse of 2008. The mother of all meltdowns is coming soon and I know exactly when this will happen. When? It

---

22 https://hallsofkarma.wordpress.com/2016/02/04/
donald-trump-vs-the-bilderberg-group-global-showdown-exposed-videos/

will happen when the string-pulling orchestrators and merchants of chaos are good and ready. In my opinion this could be later in 2019 or perhaps in 2020 or a bit beyond, but it's coming.

As I mentioned earlier, I had a successful career as a financial advisor and later as a consultant that spanned nearly fifteen years, focusing on estate planning, wealth preservation, and retirement planning. For many years we were able to use both technical and fundamental analyses as helpful tools in the design and planning process. This is now almost meaningless. With this being a completely rigged and controlled system, most technical and fundamental advice matters little.

Now some may argue this and defend their position, indicating all kinds of "proof" supporting their point, software, charts, etc – so be it. However, all of that, regardless of such analysis, can (and will) change on a dime with no notice and then it's too late. Feed the greed? Fear the fear? Or plan according to the writing on the wall. So, what to do?

Of course, I am not providing any specific advice here, as each person's situation varies and planning is based upon many criteria. So, where to begin?

I think it is most important to understand our world, as we are now witnessing yet another transition of power, this time and perhaps for the first time from Globalism back to Americanism or Nationalism. Trump vs. the NWO. But they have one "for sure bet" to take Trump and the movement to its knees, and that is to collapse the markets, collapse the economy.

Denial

We must stop and take a look around to reassess ourselves, others, life, and the systems and structures that make this world go 'round. If you are tired of spinning around in the hamster wheel called your life, then it's time to look at who is spinning that wheel and what you can do to stop this circular insanity.

There are four stages of denial that keep us from making any meaningful preparations for a disaster:

» It won't happen.
» If it does happen, it won't happen to me.
» If it does happen to me, it won't be that bad.
» If it happens to me and it is that bad, there's nothing I can do to stop it anyway.

"The pessimist complains about the wind; the optimist expects it to change; the realist adjusts the sails."

— Arthur Ward

It is time to adjust the sails!

There are certain things that are presently beyond our control, so we must identify, accept, embrace, and prepare. This is not the time to be the eternal optimist and go about life as though it were business as usual, for it is not business as usual – of this you can be sure.

Nor is it time to be the eternal pessimist or bury our heads in the sand like an ostrich. It is, however, wise to practice critical thinking, do our due diligence, and to think for ourselves and perhaps create leverage within and without the system. Lest we forget the USA Debt clock?[23]

Blame it on Trump

The recent outgoing administration would have you believe that the past eight years have been prosperous, with lower unemployment and a robust stock market. Nonsense! The past eight years have been extremely difficult with regards to the economy and people's bottom lines. The Fed has kept the banking system alive and propped up the stock market at the expense of the main street economy.

This cannot continue and although Donald Trump has pledged to

---

23 http://www.usdebtclock.org/

turn this around, the fact of the matter is, this is easier said than done and will, in fact, take some time. The wheels of deceit and deception to wreck Trump's first year in office are already at play.

After over a decade of stimulus, quantitative easing, zero interest rates, and easy money for the government, banks, and corporations, and for we the people who may have borrowed some via loans and credit cards, it means that the piper needs to be paid, and a lot more than you signed up for. Remember, the Fed comes to the table with no-risk-no-skin in the game. As you recall from Chapter Four, we talked about how the debt-based system and the Fed work, the for-profit banking cartel Fed, and that is, when it's time to cash in and reap the harvest, they always do. That time is coming soon. The U.S. government will not be able to sustain these increased costs to service this debt – a debt which is $22 trillion, on the brink of $23 trillion, at the time of this writing.

What are the probable outcomes in the event of a collapse? As the fiscal nightmare intensifies and the government cannot meet its obligations, we may see pension funds go belly up, government pensions confiscated, new plans to seize control over the 401(k), 403(b), IRAs, and other retirement plans, as this has already been presented in committee as far back as 2009.

This now sets the stage for a desperate populace to allow the globalists to seize control, usher in the one-world currency, and continue on their path in the global financial reset the ruling elite have worked on for decades. Shifting the power from West to East. From weak hands (the U.S. and E.U.) to strong hands (China). President Trump faces an extraordinary challenge.

The playing field would be leveled by bringing the Western world to its knees and redirecting the jobs, wealth, and world reserve currency to a newly created global bully (China), replacing the U.S. After all, the CIA funded Chairman Mao and Prescott Bush funded Adolf Hitler, so it's not like this has not been done before. Go look it up.

The shadow government and the mainstream media will have a field day with this orchestrated collapse, using Trump as the scapegoat and by doing just what they are so effective at doing – creating the lie, spreading the disinformation, blaming it on Trump, you, me, and the movement, and continuing to fan the flames of divide and conquer. Remember the Hegelian dialectic? Problem-reaction-solution? False flag ops? Well, this is textbook. Get ready.

This *divide and conquer* will happen rather easily, as the ruling elite are already off to a great start; the nation is still heated up and incredibly divided. This can get very ugly. Even many of us in this movement will buckle and turn against Trump and turn our back against the truth. Perhaps not you or me, but many will. One reason is when you hurt the pocketbook, I mean really hurt the pocketbook, people react. Economist and trends forecaster Gerald Celente[24] says even the simple blue- or white-collar neighbor will lose it. When you lose everything and you have nothing left to lose, you "lose it"! This, of course, will have a global impact as other governments of the world like China, for example, will turn against Trump in this scenario.

For a list of President Trump's incredible accomplishments, please visit promiseskept.com.

---

[24] It's no surprise: We saw this coming, http://trendsresearch.com

Chapter Sixteen: The Global Financial Reset

What Is Happening?

THE MONETARY SYSTEM OF THIS WORLD is based upon debt and there is far too much of it. The U.S. debt alone is mathematically impossible at this stage of the game to pay it off. With the rising interest rate environment that we are now in and will be for some years to come, the clock is ticking. Today, the service on the debt (interest payments), coupled with the mandatory obligations and entitlements of the Federal Government, we must allocate over 80% of the GDP. What happens when rates rise? When interest rates double? Well, the debt service increases. We are perhaps a few short years away from a financial collapse. Yes, Trump's economic policies are working, but this will take time. Many years in fact. We simply are running out of time.

President Trump cannot MAGA unless we seize control of our currency from the Federal Reserve, the IMF and the Rothschild banking dynasty and begin to restore sound money. Dangerous. Easier said than done but nonetheless, underway.

In addition to the debt crisis, the stock market is poised for many reasons for a serious correction and most economists the world over agree this could be far worse than the collapse of 2008-2009. Safer investments like bonds, for example, are also the wrong place to be at this time due to rising interest rates as bond yields fall when interest rates rise.

There are a series of related articles that I have written on this subject on the blog section of my website www.JohnMichaelChambers. com. Go to archives and click on "Financial".

In short, the President will seize control over the corrupt debt-based monetary and Central Banking system which includes first exercising control over the Federal Reserve before restructuring or perhaps nationalizing the Fed. Check out H.R. 24 and H.R. 25 which are essentially bills to audit the Fed and go after the I.R.S. In the end, if successful, the power will shift from the debt-based digital fiat currency system controlled by the ruling elite bankers, and restore sound money and power to the people. Gold will play a part in the backing of the currency. This battle and these transitions have already begun, and will perhaps go on for a couple of more years. This will become one of the biggest stories of the century and will begin to unfold and hit mainstream news later in 2020 and beyond. Be prepared.

Signs the Global Financial Reset has Begun

The following brief summary written by Economist Kirk Elliott, PhD, is an overview of the Global Financial Reset that is unfolding. This will be an epic historic event that one needs to prepare for.

I recently read an article by market analysts Jim Willie. He is a brilliant analyst, and I wanted to pull out a few things from his research that stood out to me in regards to a global financial reset. I went back to the source documents behind some of his projections and I concur with his analysis. Links to the source documents are provided below.

After an economic recession/depression, DEBT IS ALWAYS REDUCED. In the US, the recession of 2009 did not eliminate debt, in fact the opposite – IT EXPLODED, not just in the U.S., but globally. In fact, debt has been exploding since then and REAL GDP has been CONTRACTING by -2 to -4% a year in real terms according to John Williams of Shadow Stats.

SOURCE: https://www.silverdoctors.com/headlines/world-news/ jim-willie-the-global-currency-reset-has-begun-now-watch-these-two-key-events/

CIPS (Cross Border Interbank Payment System (started Oct 2015)), but is now gaining much momentum. Now commands $6-$8 TRILLION portfolio of funded projects. This is designed to replace the SWIFT system in the eastern hemisphere.

SOURCE: https://en.wikipedia.org/wiki/Cross-Border_Inter-Bank_Payments_System

MARCH 2018 – the Chinese rolled out a new gold-backed yuan oil contract next month as part of its attempt to replace the U.S. dollar's dominance of that commodity trade. This could spell the end of the petro dollar trade. This built-in demand for the US$ is pretty much all the demand there is for it. In time, the dollar sinks, and an alternative petro-dollar HAS ALREADY BEEN FORMED – no need to even speculate.

SOURCE: https://seekingalpha.com/article/4148232-yes-petro-yuan -threat-u-s-dollar

BRICS 2.0. By this time, everyone is aware of the BRICS nations and the coalition to form a strength-based union to counteract the west. BRICS 2.0 is that movement on steroids. Gold is one of the last commodities controlled by the west (NY and LONDON exchanges). This initiative will co-align the BRICS nations to replace that as well. This, in my opinion, is not a bad thing, as London has allowed naked shorts on futures contracts of metals for a long time, thus limiting the growth through manipulation. People who own gold and continue to acquire it should benefit AMAZINGLY as a true market will be established without the manufactured suppression of prices.

Sadly, for us as Americans, this one is on us. Our regulators allowed the manipulation to happen, and people seek truth and transparency. This is another nail in the coffin of U.S. financial dominance. SOURCE: https://www.miningreview.com/brics-gold-new -model-multilateral-cooperation/

What to Look for Moving Forward for Further Signals

According to market analyst Jim Willie, he has categorized upcoming triggers that would indicate that a global financial reset will be here before any of us could possibly imagine. Look out for any of these events:

List of Potential Key Events
Very Serious Major Global Game Changers

» Deutsche Bank failure, talk of restructure, with rupture of derivative complex.
» Italian banking system collapse, complete with numerous bank runs.
» Italian sovereign currency announced as new Lira currency in EU exit.
» London Metals Exchange launches RMB-based metals contracts.
» COMEX & LBMA rupture from lost control of integration with oil & currencies.
» Formal launch of Gold Trade Note atop the Shanghai G-O-R contracts.
» Saudi oil sales in RMB to China, adopted by other Arabs and other Asians.
» London flips East, with RMB Hub development, following their AII Bank membership.

Deep Impact Disruptions

» Flourishing non-USD platforms, led by Chinese design and efforts.

» Germans and French formally end Russian sanctions, thus flipping East.

» CIPS bank transaction system gains wider adoption, even among Western nations.

» BRICS Gold Platform announces conversion of sovereign bonds to Gold.

» China pre-announces gold-backed Yuan in the form of convertible Gold Trade Notes.

» China announced Yuan backed by basket of currencies, Gold, other commodities.

» Introduction of a new IMF SDR basket that includes gold, crude oil, and iron.

» EU opens door to Euro payments in external trade with trading partners.

» Emerging markets rupture on debt defaults, due to currency crisis.

» NATO fractures in the open and EU pursues independent military security.

SOURCE: https://www.silverdoctors.com/headlines/world-news/jim-willie-the-global-currency-reset-has-begun-now-watch-these-two-key-events/

The time is now to prepare and safeguard your assets. Please visit the final pages of this book under "Resources" to help you to navigate through this paradigm shift in monetary policy.

CHAPTER SEVENTEEN: BATTLE BEGINS – IMMIGRATION

OVER THE YEARS, WITH THE OPEN BORDERS POLICY, catch and release coupled with an influx of refugees, the demographic landscape and the face of America are changing. Trump faced enormous backlash and out-of-context reporting when it came to the border issue and immigration. The figures below are just the economic reasons *alone* why the borders must be protected, and they do not include the rapes, assaults, murders, drugs, and other related problems. In my opinion, there are five main reasons that President Trump is relentlessly attacked with regards to safeguarding the border.

1. Illegals tend to vote for Democrats. The porous border ensures an increasing pool of votes for Democrats.
2. Drug money is made at the border.
3. Gun running. Remember Fast and Furious? Gun running comes through the border.
4. Human trafficking and the child sex trade. This is big business once again coming across our borders.

5. The North American Union and the loss of US sovereignty.
   As there was the European Union and the Euro, there was
   to be the North American Union and the Amero. Canada,
   US and Mexico was to become like the EU. A borderless
   nation with one shared currency.

The following stats were excerpted from the McAlvany Intelligence
Advisor, April 2016 issue:

» 11 to 22 billion dollars are spent on welfare to illegal aliens
  each year by state governments.

» 22 billion dollars a year are spent on food assistance programs such as food stamps, WIC, and free school lunches for
  illegal aliens.

» 2.5 billion dollars a year are spent on Medicaid for illegal
  aliens.

» 12 billion dollars a year are spent on primary and secondary
  school education for children here illegally, and most cannot
  speak a word of English.

» 17 billion dollars a year are spent for education for the
  American-born children of illegal aliens, known as anchor
  babies.

» 3 million dollars a day are spent to incarcerate illegal aliens.

» 30% of all federal prison inmates are illegal aliens.

» 90 billion dollars a year are spent on illegal aliens for welfare
  and social services by the American taxpayers.

» 200 billion dollars a year in suppressed American wages are
  caused by the illegal aliens.

» In 2006, illegal aliens sent home $45 billion in remittances to
  their countries of origin.

» The dark side of illegal immigration: nearly one million sex
  crimes committed by illegal immigrants in the United States.

Visit One AMericaNews.com for a live ticker on the current cost of illegal immigration. We are on track to exceed well over $200 billion for the year!

The Great Wall of Trump

"Build that wall, build that wall, build that wall. And who is going to pay for it? Mexico!"

We all know that Donald Trump wants to keep our borders open to aliens, but they must come in legally. I am simply flabbergasted that anyone who loves America would disagree with this. I, for one, have traveled and lived in many countries, and believe me, they are strict on border control and monitoring their visitors. Like Trump has said, Mexico, to cite but one country, is one of the most difficult countries to become a citizen of. It's a circus and a free-for-all here in the U.S.

Michael Savage has dedicated the better part of the past twenty-two years to the subject of borders, language, and culture. He says these three words best describe what defines a nation, and I believe most would agree. We have allowed these things to be destroyed over the past few decades from Clinton to Bush to Obama. This will now change.

Donald Trump blasted on the scene in June 2015 at Trump Tower in New York City, and one of the very first issues he brought front and center which now echoes throughout the world is immigration and building the wall that Mexico will pay for. Trump has gone on to say in his many rally speeches across America that if you don't have borders, you don't have a country. He has referred to the effectiveness of the Great Wall of China being 13,000 miles long and having been built about 2,000 years ago. He has gone on to illustrate the effectiveness of the wall separating Israel from Palestine. And Trump says it's high time to build a wall, have Mexico pay for it, and revamp border security and immigration policies. I take him on his word.

Why so much border backlash? I mean, have we forgotten that Jimmy Carter had a ban on Iraqi Muslims in the 1970s for the safety of the country? You see, one of the reasons to keep the borders so porous is that big money is being made through the drug cartel and human trafficking issues. Also, this is where we get our "anchor baby" traffic, not to mention terrorists who are now killing us on our own soil. Another reason, and this is the key reason in my opinion, that the borders are wide open is that there are to be *no borders* between Mexico, Canada, and the U.S. in the future in accordance with Global Governance and the New World Order. This is also known as the North American Union and UN Agenda 2030 plans.

Canada, U.S., and Mexico are to be joined with perhaps a regional currency once the Globalists let the U.S. dollar collapse. This is known as the North American Union[1] and the Amero.[2] Go look it up. There are plenty of facts to support this statement. As there is (soon to be was) the European Union and the Euro, perhaps there will be the North American Union and the Amero? Not on Trump's watch.

But now things are changing. BREXIT was a big blow to the NWO and now we have President Trump and his extraordinary leadership. With a Donald Trump presidency, this puts a stop to this right away. And this is why Trump has been vilified and called a racist and a tyrant by all the frantic enemies who consider him a threat to the world order agenda and to their control and their pocketbooks. Building this wall and revamping border patrol and immigration policies will continue to come under heavy fire. I wonder if George Clooney's front door is open?

---

1 https://en.wikipedia.org/wiki/North_American_Union
2 Lou Dobbs reports on the emerging "North American Union". It's real, it's happening! https://www.youtube.com/watch?v=UW_NBLaO6Ew

My Front Door

This closing section was contributed to my blogsite by Dr. Richard Davis, MD.

Ever since I was a kid, I lived in a house fitted with a front door and a lock. That door was put there for a reason – to keep uninvited things out – bad weather, squirrels, vagrants, and anything else that might be potentially dangerous. In fact, every home that I have ever seen has a front door. I guess everybody wants to keep bad things out too. Welcome to my front door.

Is our nation any less important than our home? So why is everyone so upset with Mr. Trump for saying we need to protect our borders to keep potentially dangerous uninvited guests out of our country? Forget the propaganda, here is what Mr. Trump actually said on December 5, 2015: *"We need a total and complete shutdown of Muslims entering the United States until our country's representatives can figure out what is going on."*

The mainstream media immediately began a smear campaign labeling Mr. Trump "a racist," a bigot," an "Islamophobe" and every other disparaging name imaginable. There is only one small problem with this characterization. The Donald was right; and you agree with him. Yes, you do.

According to the best information available, approximately 85% of the "migrant population" are not Syrian families seeking asylum, as the mainstream media would have you believe, but rather they are military-age men coming in from war-torn areas all over the Middle East.

Add to this fact that a 2015 survey conducted by the Center for Security Policy found that one-quarter of U.S. Muslim respondents believed that violence against Americans (including suicide bombings) was justified as part of global jihad and that a slim majority "agreed that Muslims in America should have the choice of being governed according to Sharia [Law]." This means that approximately one in four of these migrants who are streaming across our borders have been *radicalized* to believe that God has called on them to purify the Earth of anyone who is not a true believer in Muhammed. Governor Bobby Jindal is quoted as saying: "Immigration, without assimilation, is invasion."

President Teddy Roosevelt said it another way: "We should insist that if the immigrant who comes here does in good faith become an American and assimilates himself to us, he shall be treated on an exact equality with everyone else, for it is an outrage to discriminate against any such man because of creed or birthplace or origin. But this is predicated upon the man's becoming in very fact an American and nothing but an American.

If he tries to keep segregated with men of his own origin and separated from the rest of America, then he isn't doing his part as an American.

There can be no divided allegiance here. We have room for but one language here, and that is the English language, for we intend to see that the crucible turns our people out as Americans, of American nationality, and not as dwellers in a polyglot boarding-house; and we have room for but one sole loyalty, and that is loyalty to the American people."

To put all of this into a context everyone can understand, Obama's immigration policy is like greenlighting a swarm of Stone Age people pouring through your front door with 25% of them hell-bent on killing you and your family the first chance they get. Do you support that? Mr. Trump simply wants to close the door until we can develop a way of determining who is our friend from who is our enemy. I ask you; is that racism, or bigotry, or just good common sense?

Mr. Trump just wants America to be safe. That's it. Nothing more. Hillary, on the other hand, wanted to increase the flow of these people by 550%. WTF. I mean, really; that is insane. However, out of my civic duty for tolerance and trendiness, I propose an experiment to gather the facts: anyone who supports Ms. Clinton with this idea needs to show their support by removing the front door of their home so anyone can come in. Then we'll see how well that works out for you. What? What's that you say? No? You don't want to do that? Oh. Okay. Then nothing more needs to be said. [End of post]

And now, yet another aspect of immigration as we take on the Muslim issue at the border and already within the country.

Islamization of America

It is only Donald Trump who has been brave enough to take on this issue and pledges to restore our Judeo-Christian roots while welcoming legal, law-abiding people of all faiths if elected. The following is an excerpt taken from the McAlvany Intelligence Advisor, May 2016 issue.

Before Obama there was virtually no noticeable presence of Islam in America, but then all of a sudden we must allow prayer rugs everywhere and allow for Islamic prayer in schools, airports, and businesses.

» All of a sudden we must stop serving pork in prisons.
» All of a sudden we are inundated with lawsuits by Muslims who are offended by American culture.
» All of a sudden Muslims are suing employers and refusing to do their jobs if they personally deem it conflicts with Sharia Law.

All of a sudden…

» All of a sudden the Attorney General of the United States vows to prosecute anyone who engages in "anti-Muslim speech."
» All of a sudden Muslim training compounds are popping up throughout the USA.
» All of a sudden Jihadists, who engage in terrorism and

openly admit they acted in the name of Islam and ISIS, are emphatically declared NOT Islamic by our leaders, and/or their actions are determined to not be terrorism but some other nebulous thing like "workplace violence."

All of a sudden...

» All of a sudden white men are declared to be the greatest terror threat to the country by our leaders, even while ISIS and Al Qaeda promise attacks inside the USA.

» All of a sudden it becomes U.S. policy that secular Middle East dictators, who were benign or friendly to the West, must be replaced by fundamentalist Muslims and the Muslim Brotherhood.

» All of a sudden America has reduced its nuclear stockpiles to 1950 levels, as Obama's stated goal of a nuke-free America by the time he leaves office continues uninterrupted.

» All of a sudden a deal with Iran must be made at any cost, with a pathway to nuclear weapons and hundreds of billions of dollars handed over to fund their programs.

» All of a sudden America apologizes to Muslim states and sponsors of terror worldwide for acts of aggression, war, and sabotage they perpetrate against our soldiers.

» All of a sudden the American Navy is diminished to 1917 pre-World War I levels of only 300 ships. The Army is at pre-1940 levels. The Air Force scraps 500 planes and plans to retire the use of the A-10 Thunderbolt close air support fighter. A further draw down of another 40,000 military personnel is in progress.

» All of a sudden half of our aircraft carriers are recalled for maintenance by Obama, rendering the Atlantic unguarded – none are in the Middle East.

And all of a sudden...

» All of a sudden Islam is taught in schools. Christianity and the Bible are banned in schools.

» All of a sudden Obama has to empty Guantanamo Bay of captured jihadists and let them loose in jihad-friendly Islamic states or bring them to America.

» All of a sudden America negotiated with terrorists and traded five Taliban commanders for a deserter and Jihad sympathizer.

» All of a sudden there is no money for poor, disabled, jobless, or displaced Americans, but there is endless money for Obama's "Syrian refugee" resettlement programs.

» All of a sudden Obama fills the federal government with Muslims in key positions.

» All of a sudden the most important thing for Obama to do after a mass shooting by two jihadists is to disarm American citizens.

Chapter Eighteen: Battle Begins – Political Correctness

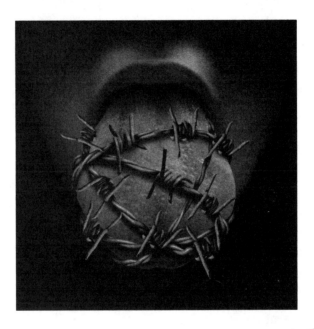

How much has political correctness contributed to the current state of affairs in the U.S.? How much have inter-relations changed between us all? Political correctness taken to the point where we find it today is really nothing more than an assault against free speech. I would take this one step further and say it is also an unwanted invasion directly against your free will, an uninvited intruder right into the heart of your spirit of who you are. Political correctness (PC) is an assault on your mind, which you are now afraid to speak. As Charlton Heston once said, "Political correctness is just tyranny with manners."

Just think about how many times you now bite your tongue in fear of offending someone or being suspected of a hate crime. George Orwell's *1984*, written in 1948, is well represented today in 2016 and getting significantly worse via executive orders and what some may say are unconstitutional laws. Libertarians (and rightly so) are up in arms about PC, considering this an attack against one's personal liberties and rights. Then there is the wonderful World Wide Web, Facebook, Google, and Microsoft, who are working hand-in-hand with the new global agenda and are rapidly becoming the control centers of what can and cannot be communicated.

This insanity has led us to things such as "hate crimes" and "tolerance" and increasing censorship on the Internet, for example.

Now, I am not advocating any form of hate or violence. I am actually a peaceful, loving man as reflected by my actions and relations and in my writings and in my book *Misconceptions and Course Corrections,* but I think you get the idea. And if you don't get the idea, maybe this article[1] will help to illustrate my point: The once great New York City will now fine you $250,000 for "misgendering" a transsexual. With all these attacks on free speech, I am sure we have made Chairman Mao most pleased.

So, this concludes but a handful of issues that will be fought upon the battlefield as we fight for our freedom from the tyrannical lunatics who are hell-bent on destroying civilization as we know it. These battles must be won, as the second American Revolution has just begun, and so, the globalists tremble as Trump threatens totalitarianism world government.

---

1 http://www.breitbart.com/tech/2015/12/27/
   nyc-will-fine-you-250000-for-misgendering-a-transsexual/

CHAPTER NINETEEN: THE TRUMP PHENOMENON

THE INAUGURATION OF DONALD J. TRUMP 45th PRESID

NEVER UNDERESTIMATE WHAT ONE MAN CAN do. The effect that Donald Trump is having can never really be fully and quantitatively measured. Why? Because it is impossible to measure the unlimited potential and power of waking up (the suppressed) human spirit. And in this case, waking up the human spirit within hundreds of millions of people (if not more) and not only in America but throughout the world. Never underestimate what one man can do.

The message, ideals, and platform of Donald J. Trump is in direct conflict of the ruling power elites' long-sought-after goal of complete global dominance via sovereign-less nations enslaving mankind. Some consider Trump's efforts a "peaceful counter revolution" or an "overthrow of the new order" when actually all that is taking place is a man trying to restore the Constitutional Republic and rebuild a once great nation in this new and dangerous world.

Although we live in increasingly and desperately dangerous times, there is a light at the end of the tunnel. The truth is *you* are the light at the end of the tunnel, and that light within us all has been turned on. We have this chance in this brief breath and moment in history to reset mankind out from the darkness and back into the light as Trump leads us in America's second revolution.

What One Man Can Do

Donald J. Trump is an absolute phenomenon. Should the full length and term(s) of his presidency be denied him in any way, shape, or form, he has already served humanity in ways comparable (in my opinion) with other natural and brave leaders whose presence inspired the masses in a positive way. These people include President Abraham Lincoln, President John F. Kennedy, Senator Robert F. Kennedy, Dr. Martin Luther King Jr., Princess Diana, Gandhi, and yes, even John Lennon.

What we see happening before us with Donald Trump has never happened before in history, and the timing is by no accident. This is America's last stand. No Trump, no hope.

These are perilous and dangerous times. Donald Trump is such a threat to the globalist ruling elite that the Republican and Democrat parties (the "Demicans" and "Republicrats" coined by Michael Savage), the media, and global leaders who stand to lose in a Trump administration are going berserk.

We must unite. Wake up your fellow man. Share this book every-where right now. Surround yourself with like-minded people who do truly understand the times in which we live and strengthen and grow those circles. We must stay strong as a people, and know that the light of God is shining down upon us.

On the subject of tyrannical governments, Thomas Jefferson back in the day said, "I hold it that a little rebellion now and then is a good thing, and as necessary in the political world as storms in the physical." One could say of the Trump phenomenon and the movement that was created that what we have is a peaceful overthrow of the U.S. government. Jefferson would be proud.

Peaceful Overthrow of the U.S. Government – Jefferson Would Be Proud

Governor Mike Huckabee has called the "Trump Revolution" a popular revolt against the ruling class. In an interview with Newsmax TV, Huckabee said, "Here is a guy who has said some very inflammatory, very intemperate things, and rather than it hurt him, it has actually propelled him because that's how people feel." Huckabee went on to say that "People are angry. I think we're seeing nothing less than the overthrow of our government. It's a peaceful overthrow so far. We're going to do it by ballots, not bullets, thank God, but this is a revolution. The people are that upset with the ruling class, and frankly, they ought to be." On this subject, I agree with Huckabee, and he was right as we won at the ballot box!

The attacks and danger will continue, but President Trump now has some degree of control, holding the most powerful office in the world. And he is not alone, as many other leaders will emerge (and are already doing so today) from around the globe in support of freedom versus tyranny. Leaders like Vladimir Putin for example. He will also have the support of the majority of people.

"Rebellion to tyrants is obedience to God."

— Thomas Jefferson

A Voice from the Past

Back in 1999, I came across Washington's Three Visions from a pamphlet that the St. Germain Foundation out of Mt. Shasta, California, had printed. This originally came from a newspaper article first published in the *National Tribune* in 1859 and reprinted in 1880 (vol. 4, no. 12, Dec. 1880).

The vision was related to a reporter named Wesley Bradshaw by an officer who served under General Washington at Valley Forge, named Anthony Sherman. This is the recorded testimony of Wesley Bradshaw's encounter with Anthony Sherman, who has claimed the firsthand story told to him by George Washington. This is "Washington's Vision Three Is Upon Us." These visions were so inspiring to me that I wrote a song back in 1999 titled "Valley Forge."

In the vision, Washington sees three great trials to overtake the Union. These were the Revolutionary War, the Civil War, and the greatest threat, a war fought on the soil of the United States as the final conflict. These are the words of a firsthand observer, Anthony Sherman, who was there and describes the situation: "You doubtless heard the story of Washington's going to the thicket to pray. Well, it is not only true, but he used to often pray in secret for aid and comfort from God, the interposition of whose Divine Providence brought us safely through the darkest days of tribulation."

Washington's Vision Number Three Is Upon Us

"One day, I remember it well, when the chilly winds whistled through the leafless trees, though the sky was cloudless and the sun shone brightly, he remained in his quarters nearly all the afternoon alone. When he came out, I noticed that his face was a shade paler than usual. There seemed to be something on his mind of more than ordinary importance. Returning just after dusk, he dispatched an orderly to the quarters of the officer I mention, who was presently in attendance. After a preliminary conversation of about a half hour, Washington, gazing upon his companion with that strange look of dignity which he alone commanded, related the events that occurred that day. And now this from General George Washington...

"This afternoon, as I was sitting at the table engaged in preparing a dispatch, something seemed to disturb me. Looking up, I beheld standing opposite me a singularly beautiful female. So astonished was I, for I had given strict orders not to be disturbed, that it was some moments before I found language to inquire the cause of her presence.

A second, a third and even a fourth time did I repeat my question, but received no answer from my mysterious visitor except a slight raising of her eyes. By this time, I felt strange sensations spreading through me. I would have risen, but the riveted gaze of the being before me rendered volition impossible. I assayed once more to address her, but my tongue had become useless, as though it had become paralyzed.

A new influence, mysterious, potent, and irresistible, took possession of me. All I could do was to gaze steadily, vacantly, at my unknown visitor. Gradually the surrounding atmosphere seemed as if it had become filled with sensations and luminous. Everything about me seemed to rarefy, the mysterious visitor herself becoming more airy and yet more distinct to my sight than before. I now began to feel as one dying, or rather to experience the sensations which I have sometimes imagined accompany dissolution. I did not think, I did not reason, I did not move; all were alike, impossible. I was only conscious of gazing fixedly, vacantly at my companion.

Presently I heard a voice saying, 'Son of the Republic, look and learn,' while, at the same time, my visitor extended her arm eastward. I now beheld a heavy white vapor at some distance rising fold upon fold.

This gradually dissipated, and I looked upon a strange scene. Before me lay spread out in one vast plain all the countries of the world – Europe, Asia, Africa, and America. I saw rolling and tossing between Europe and America the billows of the Atlantic and between Asia and America the Pacific.

'Son of the Republic,' said the mysterious voice as before, 'look and learn.' At that moment I beheld a dark shadowy being, like an angel, standing, or rather floating in midair between Europe and America. Dipping water out of the ocean in the hollow of each hand, he sprinkled some upon America with his right hand, while, with his left hand, he cast some on Europe. Immediately a cloud raised from these countries and joined in mid-ocean. For a while it remained stationary and then moved slowly westward, until it enveloped America in its murky folds. Sharp flashes of lightning gleamed through it at intervals, and I heard the smothered groans and cries of the American people.

A second time the angel dipped water from the ocean and sprinkled it out as before. The dark cloud was then drawn back to the ocean, in whose heaving bellows it sank from view. A third time I heard the mysterious voice saying, 'Son of the Republic, look and learn.' I cast my eyes upon America and beheld villages and towns and cities springing up one after another until the whole land from the Atlantic to the Pacific was dotted with them.

Again, I heard the mysterious voice say, 'Son of the Republic, the end of the century cometh. Look and learn.' At this, the dark shadowy angel turned his face southward and, from Africa, I saw an ill-omened specter approach our land. It flitted slowly over every town and city of the latter.

The inhabitants presently set themselves in battle array against each other. As I continued looking, I saw a bright angel, on whose brow rested a crown of light on which was traced 'Union,' bearing the American which he placed between the divided nation and said, 'Remember ye are brethren.' Instantly, the inhabitants, casting aside from them their weapons became friends once more and united around the National Standard.

And again I heard the mysterious voice saying, 'Son of the Republic, look and learn.' At this, the dark shadowy angel placed a trumpet to his mouth and blew three distinct blasts; and taking water from the ocean he sprinkled it upon Europe, Asia, and Africa. Then my eyes beheld a fearful scene: from each of these countries arose thick black clouds that were soon joined into one. Throughout this mass there gleamed a dark red light by which I saw hordes of armed men, who, moving with the cloud, marched by land and sailed by sea to America. Our country was enveloped in this volume of cloud and I saw these vast armies devastate the whole country and burn the villages, towns, and cities that I beheld springing up. As my ears listened to the thundering of the cannon, clashing of swords, and the shouts and cries of millions in mortal combat, I heard the mysterious voice saying, 'Son of the Republic, look and learn.' When the voice had ceased, the dark shadowy angel placed his trumpet once more to his mouth and blew a long and fearful blast.

Instantly, a light as of a thousand suns shone down from above me and pierced and broke into fragments the dark cloud which enveloped America. At the same time, the angel upon whose head still shone the word Union, and who bore our national flag in one hand and a sword in the other, descended from the heavens attended by legions of white spirits. These immediately joined the inhabitants of America, who I perceived were nigh well overcome, but who immediately taking courage again, closed up their broken ranks and renewed the battle.

Again, amid the fearful noise of the conflict, I heard the mysterious voice saying, 'Son of the Republic, look and learn.' As the voice ceased, the shadowy angel for the last time dipped water from the ocean and sprinkled it upon America. Instantly, the dark cloud rolled back, together with the armies it had brought, leaving the inhabitants of the land victorious. Then once more I beheld the villages, towns, and cities springing up where I had seen them before, while the bright angel, planting the azure standard he had brought in the midst of them, cried with a loud voice: 'While the stars remain and the heavens send down dew upon the earth, so long shall the Union last.' And taking from his brow the crown on which blazoned the word 'Union,' he placed it upon the Standard while the people, kneeling down, said, 'Amen.'

The scene instantly began to fade and dissolve, and I at last saw nothing but the rising, curling vapor I at first beheld. This also disappearing, I found myself once more gazing upon the mysterious visitor, who said in the same voice I had heard before, 'Son of the Republic, what you have seen is thus interpreted: three great perils will come upon the Republic. The most fearful is the third, but in this greatest conflict the whole world united shall not prevail against her. Let every child of the Republic learn to live for his God, his land, and the Union.' With these words the vision vanished and I started from my seat and felt that I had seen a vision wherein had been shown to me the birth, progress, and destiny of the United States."

Thus ended General George Washington's vision and prophecy for the United States of America as told in his own words.

In my opinion, as George Washington was divinely inspired and protected to form America, it is my belief that Donald Trump is divinely inspired and protected to resurrect America, thus the title of this book, "Trump and the Resurrection of America".

America's Last Stand

With all the issues concerning America and the human race, we may also learn a bit from Alexander Tytler. The original concept of the Cycle of Democracy leads us to Dr. Alexander Tytler, a Scottish professor who wrote a scholarly tome from which this concept comes, called *The Athenian Republic*. This was published shortly before the thirteen American colonies gained independence from Britain. If you do additional research, you will find that his students and other sources over the years contributed to the "Cycle of Democracy."

This body of work states that a democracy cannot exist as a permanent form of government. It can only exist until the voters discover they can vote themselves generous gifts from the public treasury. From that moment on, the majority always vote for the candidates who promise them the most benefits from the public treasury, with the result that democracy will collapse over loose fiscal policy, which is always followed by a dictatorship. Sound familiar, America? Careful who you vote for.

Cycle of Democracy

The average age of the world's greatest civilizations has been approximately 200 years. These nations rise and fall and have progressed through this sequence.

- » Bondage to spiritual faith
- » Spiritual faith to courage
- » Courage to liberty
- » Liberty to abundance
- » Abundance to selfishness
- » Selfishness to apathy
- » Apathy to dependency
- » Dependency back into bondage

It is often said that unless we learn from the lessons of history, we are destined to repeat it. Therefore, we will begin by taking a brief stroll through history so that we can identify the similarities and the specific occurrences from a broad perspective in the "Cycle of Democracy" that took place in nations throughout history.

We'll do this so that we may be prepared for the immediate dangers that this presents, as well as identifying the new trends and opportunities that arise during such transitions.

Those who stay informed, do their due diligence, and take decisive action, may reap the benefits. Be prepared as the global markets may once again decimate the wealth of the people until the Global Financial Reset settles in. When? Perhaps any time now in 2019 or 2020 in this one man's opinion. It is not a matter of *if,* but rather a matter of *when.*

We begin with understanding the fact that nothing lasts forever.

Nothing stays the same. In our universe, things expand and contract, and this applies to the birth and death of nations and civilizations. There are many examples of this throughout history.

It is within this cycle where we can identify these changes that have taken place throughout history and are indeed taking place today in many parts of the world, with the greatest impact here in the United States of America, Canada, and Europe. During the previous century, the financial power has centered on the Western world, in the U.S. and in Europe. This is changing…and changing rapidly.

This shift of power will expose the masses to significant dangers as well as opportunities. The rise and fall of nations have occurred many times throughout history. Here are but a few examples: British Empire,[1] Roman Empire,[2] Ottoman Empire,[3] Ming Dynasty,[4] and Qing Dynasty.[5]

The Resurrection of America

I would submit to you that the United States has been, for many recent years, at the stage of "apathy to dependency." But now, as of January 20, 2017, with the inauguration of Donald J. Trump, the spirit of true hope and optimism has returned to America and the world. We can reverse this dwindling spiral – we must, we can, and we will, as we are returning to "spiritual faith leading us to great courage" so we can unite and restore this once great republic via this second American revolution.

The resurrection of America, in my opinion, will not happen without the grace of God. We have been given this chance, but we – each and every one of us – must do our part in supporting our new leadership in Washington D.C. Donald Trump and his administration need

---

1 https://en.wikipedia.org/wiki/British_Empire
2 https://en.wikipedia.org/wiki/Roman_Empire
3 https://en.wikipedia.org/wiki/Ottoman_Empire
4 https://en.wikipedia.org/wiki/Ming_dynasty
5 https://en.wikipedia.org/wiki/Qing_dynasty

to be on high alert, as no doubt he will be infiltrated from within and given faulty intelligence and other such tactics to derail his agenda's progress, to attempt to utterly discredit him, and to have the people turn against him. It has been reported that President Trump has hired his own security force in addition to the Secret Service. This is wise, as the enemy often strikes from within.

Yes, President Trump will have to play politics here and there, as this is par for the course, but President Trump needs to implement bold and swift action and go for the jugular right away in order to gain the upper hand, which he (we) does not have right now by any stretch of the imagination. This soon may change. Are you going to support President Trump? Are you prepared to do whatever it takes to save this country?

CHAPTER TWENTY: TRUMPING GLOBAL GOVERNANCE

What If?

WHAT IF THE U.S. CONSTITUTION was no longer applicable? What if the United States began to resemble an oligarchy? What if a President could bypass Congress and declare war on his or her own? What if the government could read your emails and texts without a search warrant, or monitor and control your calls, purchases, Internet searches, social media postings, and essentially every move in your life? What if the President could kill you without warning?

What if a private bank seized control over the issuance of a country's money supply? What if U.S. Supreme Court justices referred to previous justices rather than the U.S. Constitution? What if the states were no longer sovereign states? What if your government did not protect its language, borders, and culture? What if the nation, due to bad trade policy and poor budget management, created an unsustainable debt exceeding $19 trillion? What if a nation started unfunded wars costing the lives of millions and costing the taxpayers trillions without ever "winning"? What if a nation's veterans were unable to receive adequate healthcare upon returning from the battlefield? What if you needed a license to speak, assemble, or protest against the government? What if the right to keep and bear arms belonged only to the government? What if we no longer had a free press? What if the U.S. allowed hundreds of billions of dollars in trade deficits with foreign nations each and every year? What if a nation created a 24% unemployment level and lied to the people, stating that it was only 5%? What if our healthcare system was out of control, expensive, and about to implode?

What if the U.S. Constitution was no longer the supreme law of the land and Islamic Sharia Law began to take over? What if your right to free speech was silenced via political correctness?

What if the education system costs were among the highest in the world, yet among the lowest in scores? What if a college graduate has $50,000 to $100,000 in debt and cannot find a job? What if the two-party system is a fraud and is bought and controlled, giving you the illusion you have a say in the process? What if your candidates for office are lifelong criminals and lifelong corrupt, career politicians? What if the candidates were controlled and selected, not elected? What if almost everything you knew to be true is a big fat lie? What if you were responsible for leaving behind a dangerous world void of freedom and opportunity for your children and grandchildren? What if the once greatest and most revered nation on earth was a breath away from losing its freedom and sovereignty to a New World Order?

What is it going to take to "Trump" global governance? What will it take to seize control from the tyrannical totalitarian shadow government? How can we put an end to the police state we are now subject to? We can do this by first understanding the broad issues that need redirecting and by bold, swift moves ensuring victory from the clutches of evil.

Law and Order

President Trump is the law-and-order President. I am certain that President Trump will shake up business as usual in D.C. on the pathway to restoring law and order. It would be my hope that we see domestic terror groups like Black Lives Matter (along with those financing them – Soros, and Clinton, etc.) to be prosecuted and eliminated. Could Soros be considered a domestic terrorist? Seems to me he is a co-conspirator. With the FBI testimony incriminating Clinton along with the email documents from WikiLeaks on numerous people and numerous issues, President Trump and his DOJ can really shake things up. Could we see modern-day Nuremberg-style trials? This would be the ultimate "swamp draining," wouldn't you say? Could people like Eric Holder, Valerie Jarret, and many others face the firing line of a Trump DOJ? Would both Bill and Hillary face charges? How about President Obama? The Bushes? Cheney and so on? Time will tell.

So, what are some of the issues that will be addressed in this transformation back to America? What will it take to restore our Constitutional Republic and trump global governance?

The following was written by my good friend and fellow truth revealer, Dr. Richard Davis, MD.

To help make this minefield more manageable, I have attempted to analyze our choice in a rational manner.

Category	Donald Trump	Ruling Elite Globalists
Background	Political Outsider	Establishment Insiders
Career	Businessman	Politicians and Psychopaths
Political Sentiment	Nationalist	Globalists

Category	Donald Trump	Ruling Elite Globalists
Economic Policy	Free Market Capitalism	Government Controlled Centrally Planned Economy
Immigration Policy	Need to halt immigration for anyone who cannot be vetted, with special emphasis on those coming in from Muslim areas until we can establish a reliable system to assure the safety of Americans	Increase un-vetted immigration of Syrian Refugees by 550%, despite the fact that they cannot be vetted and could be radical jihadists – sworn enemies of the United States
Islamic Terrorism Policy	Believes it is our biggest threat. Would work with Russia and others to annihilate ISIS quickly	Will not even say the words or address the issue. Provided funding and support for numerous radical Islamic groups as Sec. of State, including ISIS
Build a Wall	Supports	Opposes
Banking Reform	Audit the Federal Reserve	Loosen banking regulation even more
Return of Glass-Steagall Act	Supports	Opposes
Women's Issues	Has historically provided equal pay and advancement opportunities in his 500+ corporations for over 30 years	Claims to be a women's advocate, but pays them only 83% of men in equal jobs in the Clinton Foundation. Accepts hundreds of $millions from countries that condone Sharia Law, which is the most anti-woman belief system on the planet. Supported Bill Clinton and his serial rapes, abuses, and attacks on women

Category	Donald Trump	Ruling Elite Globalists
Race Policy	Hired all races in his businesses and sued the city to allow inclusion of people of every race into his private club in Palm Beach	Has paid lip service for years pandering to the black and Hispanic communities, yet has little to show for her efforts
Russia	Sees them as a valuable potential ally and trading partner and wants peace with them	Intends to increase military pressure believing Russia to be a threat and wants to build up offensive forces against them
Foreign Policy	Believes that we should cease all nation-building escapades	Supported the wars and violent overthrow of Syria, Tunisia, Egypt, Iraq, Serbia, Ukraine, Sudan. Result: millions of innocent people have been killed
Iraq War	Opposed	Took us to war
Government Power	Wants to minimize federal government power with most authority shifted back to the states	Believes in federal government supremacy in all aspects of law
Constitution	Supreme law of the land as written, strict construction	A living document that needs to be continuously reinterpreted by the Federal Courts and Supreme Court
Government Transparency	Favors	Opposes
Police	Admires them and supports them, wants to keep them under local control	Thinks they are the problem; wants increased federalization of local police
Common Core	Abolish it	Expand it

Category	Donald Trump	Ruling Elite Globalists
Obamacare	Replace it with something less costly and more effective	Expand it
Marijuana	100% for medical marijuana, but flip-flops on legalization, currently leaning towards it	Will support rescheduling marijuana, taking a wait-and-see attitude towards legalization
Political Style	Openly discuss our problems	Deny, deny, deny, then spin that the problems do not really exist or are of minimal importance
Vouchers for School Choice	Supports	Opposes
Individual Rights	Believes that individual rights are superior to government	Believes government rights are superior
Wall Street	Refused campaign contributions and stated they are corrupt	Huge supporter and takes tens of millions of dollars in campaign contributions
Military	Supports increasing force readiness, preparedness, and technology	Will continue Obama's force reduction programs and purges, increasing use of private contractors and mercenaries and reliance on UN troops
Women in Combat	Opposed	Supports
Criminal Investigations	None	Numerous
Campaign Contributions	Self-funded primaries, now accepting donor funding	Taken upwards of $2 billion in legal and illegal contributions

Category	Donald Trump	Ruling Elite Globalists
LGBTQ	Supports equality, same-sex marriage and believes that government has no role to regulate what happens in the bedroom	Flip-flops opinion based on most recent polling data
First Amendment	Strong supporter	Wants increasing censorship of her opponents and supports SOPA/PIPA laws and other legislation to restrict Internet free speech
Second Amendment	Strong supporter, member of NRA. Believes people have the monopoly on power	Wants gun control, believes that government has the right of exclusive monopoly on power
Internet	Wants free, open, and unrestricted access and content	Wants to increase censorship and governmental controls, as well as taxing access and usage
Energy Policy	Free market approach with elimination of government controls	Shutter coal mines and coal power plants to kill jobs and increase energy costs
Prioritize Green Energy	Strongly opposes	Strongly supports
Privatize Social Security	Strongly supports	Strongly opposes
Election	Worked hard to run a clean and transparent campaign to defeat his opponents in the primary elections and had to overcome every trick in the book that was used to steal votes and delegates, including canceling of elections and RNC appointment of unelected delegates	Now facing charges of election fraud in multiple states and had hundreds of delegates replaced at the DNC with paid "seat fillers" in an effective strategy to not only steal the election from Bernie Sanders, but also to quell the legitimate angry response by his supporters to that theft

Category	Donald Trump	Ruling Elite Globalists
Allegations	Connected to a series of bankruptcies	Connected to a series of murders
UN Agenda 21, Agenda 2030	Opposes	Supports
TPP, NAFTA, GATT	Opposes	Supports
Bilderbergers	Opposes	Supports
Carbon Taxes ($100 trillion per decade to go to the 1%)	Opposes	Supports
United Nations	Opposes	Supports
Global Governance	Opposes	Supports
Counsel for Foreign Relations	Opposes	Supports
World Bank, the Bank for International Settlements, and the IMF	Opposes	Supports
Wall Street Banks Too Big to Fail	Opposes	Supports
The Electoral Process	Plays by the rules	Cheats and manipulates

[End of Dr. Davis content]

I would also highly recommend getting copies of both *Government Zero* and *Scorched Earth*[1] by Dr. Michael Savage. Savage lays out the blueprint to save America.

The following was a personal letter written by Dr. Richard Davis and delivered to then candidate Donald Trump. It has been reprinted here to raise awareness among we the people of the severity of the situation and that a bold, swift approach to seizing control over this nation and returning the control back to the people needs to occur swiftly. Perhaps we can use this as a reference point to change the narrative on social media and to see that these issues are taken up in Washington, D.C.

The Resurrection of America

Mr. Trump,

First thing after your inauguration ceremony, at 1 PM hold a mandatory-attendance webinar from the Oval Office for all federal executive branch employees. You let them know that there is a new sheriff in town, and that things are going to fundamentally change [for the better]. You let them know that from now on, the number one job of the government is to protect the natural and enumerated constitutional rights of all citizens. Everything else is secondary.

You identify that endemic corruption is the biggest problem in government and lay out a comprehensive anti-corruption plan with full whistle-blower protections, including cash rewards for identifying the "bad guys" within their departments. Provide a confidential mechanism for them to contact your Office of Anti-corruption. Let them know that those who get on board with your administration's reforms and anti-corruption measures will be rapidly promoted; those who don't will hear your famous phrase, "You're fired" (i.e., forced early retirement). This needs to happen quickly and system wide, in every

---

1 https://www.amazon.com/s/?ie=UTF8&keywords=government+zero&tag=mh0b-20&index=stripbooks&hvadid=7014431741&hvqmt=e&hvbmt=be&hvdev=c&ref=pd_sl_2z9yo6dibc_e

one of the departments that you oversee. I have some suggestions:

Executive Office of the President

Establish the Office of Anti-corruption (as above). Establish the Office of Citizen Ombudsmen, which has personnel situated within every federal department and agency to provide independent direct citizen access for redress of grievances, whistle blowing, and other activities as a redundant access portal beyond Congressional representation. Establish a series of Citizens' Investigation Commissions. Fully empowered federal grand juries, each composed of twelve experts and thirteen laymen. Full subpoena powers. Full unrestricted access to all NSA files, all government personnel, all top secret and above top secret files as needed. Witnesses are called to testify without notice and without counsel empowered to grant limited immunity in exchange for testimony.

Investigations Will Include

The 911 attacks, vaccines, geoengineering, HAARP, global warming, water fluoridation, GMO foods, Project Blue Book and Project Blue Beam and other *Disclosure* related topics, MK Ultra, "Fast and Furious," false flags, Waco, OK City bombing, Sandy Hook, Boston bombing, and others.

Assassination Commissions

JFK, RFK, MLK, Malcom X, Vince Foster, Antonin Scalia, and others.

Start a Nationalist Party

We need a true two-party system. Right now we have a one-party system. It's a charade, a shell game with no peas under either shell. As we have seen with Boehner and McConnell, we have an oligarch running America. We voted in conservatives and they were put at the back of the bus. *Conservative* has become meaningless. A Nationalist Party would attract disaffected members from both parties and tip the balance of power back to the people.

Close the Borders Completely for Seven Years

We have had unprecedented immigration into this country, not just in terms of numbers, but of foreign and even hostile cultures. We need time to assimilate the immigrants we have, just as we did the waves of immigrants at the beginning of the last century. At the end of seven years, evaluate our capacity for normalizing immigration with Nationalist priorities as I've described.

Deport All Illegal Aliens in American Prisons

That would be up to one-third of the prison population, which exceeds two million prisoners. This is not an expense the American taxpayers should be bearing, especially in a down economy.

Czars

Independent counsels that head up Public/Private Reform Commissions that gather information and submit evidence and recommendations.

Agencies

These would include the following areas of responsibility:

» AI-Robotics-Automation, balanced budget, banking, oversee transition to state.
» Chartered banks, biotechnology – nanotechnology.
» Business – oversee the breakup of all cartels and monopolies.
» Constitution – make recommendations for new amendments to secure liberty and safeguard freedoms.
» Education.
» Elections – ban political parties' control over elections and candidate selection, local election commission vetting of all candidates' qualifications for office, open primaries and general elections, one man one vote, public funding of all campaigns, duplicate voting, electronic machines – preliminary

unofficial tabulations, public ballot counting of paper ballots in each precinct for official results.

» Energy.

» Entitlements programs.

» Healthcare.

» FDA reorganization.

» Immigration.

» Infrastructure.

» Internet.

» Intelligence – place FISA court under congressional jurisdiction, eliminate all forms of warrantless collection of intelligence on U.S. citizens at home and abroad, enforce constitutional protections for all citizens.

» Judicial – oversee the full review of all legal decisions made since 1791 to determine lawfulness and Constitutionality, and then make recommendations for congressional action, review fitness of all federal judges and make recommendations for congressional impeachment and removal if necessary.

» Law enforcement.

» Legal – oversee the implementation of citizen access to present evidence directly to grand juries at federal, state, and local levels, make recommendations for all other reforms necessary to secure individual liberties.

» Public lands – disband the Bureau of Land Management and the Federal Park Service, and transfer all federal lands to the states.

» Space exploration.

» States' rights – oversee the transition of all unconstitutional federal authority to the states.

» Taxation.

Mr. Trump,

The once-invisible globalist elites have now been exposed. They are meeting this week at the Bilderberg Conference in Dresden, Germany, and are concerned that their plans to install Hillary as their next presidential puppet may not be working out as hoped. You have caught them flat-footed.

So you can bet that if they cannot prevail in rigging the election to prevent your presidency, they are busy cooking up Plan B to destroy your effectiveness once you are in office. I'm sure that it's going to be a very clever and creative, yet diabolical plan. My guess is that it will be probably a lot less messy than assassinating you outright; and will be designed to be far more effective towards achieving their centuries-long ambition of installing their utopian, unelected, one-world government – with them at the top of course.

These psychopaths have positioned the U.S., along with the rest of the world, on the brink of disaster. They are using this control position to blackmail governments and leaders of every country to do whatever they say, by threatening to unleash one or all of their doomsday weapons. They will undoubtedly try to blackmail you too. If you resist, they will work to keep you so busy by releasing bioweapons, pulling the plug on the economy with financial collapse, rolling out false flag attacks, etc., that the ensuing social chaos will force you into a martial law scenario so that none of your planned reforms could be implemented by a bought-and-paid-for Congress made up of corrupt minions of the New World Order and the totally corrupted federal bureaucracy that you will be inheriting. I have an idea for you that could change all that. You are a fighter – a counter puncher who doubles down when confronted. Perfect.

Remember, it's only the people at the top who are the "bad guys." Everyone else is either compartmentalized or psychologically entrained or both. These are good people. They will support your vision and the positive changes you have in mind, but you need their support. All you have to do is educate them, and provide leadership, support, and empowerment for them to do their jobs right. It is the same principle that you use in your businesses today.

So I Suggest the Following

The moment that you are sworn in, you will not have much time, so you need to take immediate and total operational control of the Executive Branch by enacting a series of Executive Orders that your transition team will have prepared in advance (like Obama's sealing of his records). And do it fast!!!! These orders will have the effect to make a series of sweeping and comprehensive changes in the way the Executive Branch operates. You do not need congressional or judicial authorization to do this. Obama proved this.

Judicial Branch

At 2 PM notify all judges that there will be a full investigation of all rulings over the last 100 years by your Constitutional Compliance Review Board that will make recommendations pertaining to legal and jurist reviews to ensure that all laws comport with constitutional mandates and limitations.

Legislative Branch

At 3 PM meet with a joint session of Congress to submit FastTrack legislation to rescind the unconstitutional provisions contained within the NDAA, the Patriot Act, and all other anti-American laws, and call for:

» Reinstatement of the Glass-Steagall Act
» Termination of the Affordable Care Act (Obamacare)
» Termination of the IRS
» Termination of Common Core
» Termination of the Dodd-Frank Legislation
» Introduce term limits for all elected federal positions
» Senate – three six-year terms (eighteen years)

» Congress – ten two-year terms (twenty years)

» President – two four-year terms (eight years)

The Nation

At 8 PM that evening you address the American people to:

Assure everyone that none of the bad things that they have been brainwashed to believe are going to happen will happen. But you need their help. You are not going to start WWIII; you are not going to tolerate social misfits or illegals who will not assimilate; and you have seized control of the banks and are not going to allow a financial collapse.

Speak openly about America's true enemies and your plans to bring them to justice (see below).

Assure us that anyone attempting to undermine our financial security will be charged with treason and sedition and will be tried in a military court as enemy combatants; and that there is no place on earth for them to hide from American justice.

Issue a moratorium on all bank debt repayment of any kind (mortgages, student loans, credit cards, etc.) until the banking system can be restructured and recapitalized. Assure everyone that during this transition period, no-one will starve (EBT cards will operate) or be forced from their homes. All bank accounts will remain open, no bank runs will occur, and all ATMs will operate.

All grocery stores will have food, all power will remain on. Speak openly of your entire plan so that everyone can see the big picture about what is going to happen. Use full transparency and truth to set the expectations, timelines, and challenges. Hold a press conference the next morning to announce specifics of your plan.

» Nationalize the Federal Reserve.

» Begin public issuance of currency and credit through the Department of Treasury under a new independent non-partisan agency, the Congressional Monetary Authority like

CBO, GAO, and the CRS. Establish a new non-debt-based American dollar that is real money backed by a basket of commodities: gold, silver, oil, and gas, etc.

» Restructure the large "too-big-to-fail" commercial banks into regional and state banks by re-chartering them to conform with the operations similar to the State Bank of North Dakota.

» Profits would be distributed to make up for any shortfall in funding for all federal, state and local operations in lieu of personal income taxes.

» Repudiate the national debt to foreign nations with write-downs against payments owed to us by these foreign governments for prior national defense services that we provided.

» Begin the process of repatriating the hundreds of trillions of dollars that have been stolen from the American people since 1913 (Federal Reserve Act) and use these funds to eliminate our debt (in a modified jubilee) and create citizens' savings accounts that are invested in T-Bills equal to about $1M for every citizen which will have specific use provisions to eliminate any inflationary tendencies.

» Establish free catastrophic healthcare plans and free health maintenance plans through the Public Health Service.

» Arrest the known war criminals Bushes, Clintons, Soros, Kissinger, Brzezinski, and all of the regular attendees of Bilderberg/CFR/the Bohemian Grove and any other known conspirators who seek to destroy our nation. You will know who they are from your FBI briefings and NSA files.

» Organize a fully transparent Truth and Reconciliation Tribunal to hold public hearings on a dedicated public television channel and streaming Internet site where the criminals are tried (like the Nuremberg hearings after WWII) where anyone can present evidence directly as a witness.

» Exit the UN and close the NYC headquarters.

» Announce our financial and military support for any people who choose to depose their corrupt elites as well.

» Meet with Russia and China to forge an alliance of fair trade. Announce a massive full-employment public works program designed to hire 100 million people to rebuild our infrastructure just like FDR's WPA.

» Phase out the welfare state for the able-bodied and hire them into entry level positions to service the Make America Great Plan.

» Provide OJT education, training, and advancement opportunities to turn jobs into careers with special emphasis on the following projects:

» The North American Water and Power Alliance

» Renewable Energy Initiatives

» Zero Point Energy Competition

» Complete the rebuilding of all schools, bridges, roads, levies, dams, office buildings, a new hardened power grid, airports, mass transit, high-speed rail, gardens, parks, waterways, stadiums, concert halls, sports arenas, a series of spaceports, water treatment plants, and hydroelectric facilities, etc.

» Nationwide, give free access to a high-speed Wi-Fi Internet system that uses non-toxic frequencies.

» Reassign TSA members to border security.

» Restructure our Intelligence Agencies with citizens' oversight commissions.

» Hold congressional hearings on the CIA like the Church hearings in the 1970s.

» Investigate whistleblower claims of a secret space program and a breakaway civilization.

» Place FISA court under Congressional Judiciary Committee scrutiny.

» NSA to provide investigators with all files of the elites.

» All elites' properties and financial assets to be confiscated until after their trials. If found guilty their assets will be sold at auctions.

» Overhaul education with a system of merit-based grants for all of our best schools and full scholarships for all of our brightest students.

» Begin rounding up undesirable illegals for deportation.

» De-militarize police and announce new rules of engagement for citizen interaction.

» Veterans affairs actions.

I have certainly left out a lot of excellent reforms and other good ideas that will Make America Great Again, but this is a good place to start. May you stay safe and exercise wisdom with insight to set America back on course, and pull us away from the brink of the looming tyranny and social collapse currently planned for us. Failure is simply not an option.

- Dr. Richard Davis, MD [End of Dr. Davis content]

Summary

To some these may seem like extreme measures, but this is not business as usual, and nothing about President Donald Trump is business as usual. This is the fight for our survival as a nation and for all of humanity. Extraordinary times require extraordinary measures, for the consequences of failure at this stage of the game are catastrophic.

"No task is too great. No goal is beyond our reach."

– Donald J Trump

CHAPTER TWENTY-ONE: THE DONALD IS IN DANGER

I DO NOT LIKE TO BRING THIS UP. I don't wish to bring attention to this subject, but this is another *disruptive, uncomfortable truth*. What can we do? For those of us of faith...pray.

Some don't like him as a person. Some don't like his political positions. I know two things for certain. Donald Trump is now President and Donald Trump is in danger...serious danger. I asked the following question in a blog post on my website: "What do JFK, RFK, MLK, John Lennon, Princess Diana, Gandhi, and Donald Trump have in common?" They all were a threat to the established order.[1] They each challenged the power centers within the structured and controlled establishment. They each paid the ultimate price.

The elitists and the United Nations are at the final major thrust towards global dominance via global governance, and Donald Trump is upsetting the apple cart in a very big way. He must be stopped and there are a few ways they can do this. So I ask, is the Donald in danger?

---

1 George Carlin -"Who Really Controls America," https://www.youtube.com/watch?v=hYICOeZYEtI

In this one man's opinion and if history is any indication, yes, you bet he is, serious danger. Through mind control, the shadow government and the ruling elite can easily arrange either a deranged, disgruntled Black, Mexican, or Muslim, for starters, to simply pull the trigger one day. The technology exists to create a heart attack via a satellite from space. There could be a "plane accident." The list is endless. These tactics have been going on for decades. People often ask me this important question, and I ask it of myself just the same. How is it that Trump is still alive?

How Is Trump Still Alive?

Since these psychopaths and sociopaths as described earlier on in this book can easily do away with him (and would not lose one second's sleep over it), and since this election could have been prevented, then why haven't they? The answer is we simply don't know, but we can speculate. Here are a few possible scenarios out of many:

» They're afraid of the uprising and social unrest from many armed civilians.

» They're concerned that the retired and underground ex-military and ex-CIA, ex-FBI, etc. will co-ordinate a coup d'état in conjunction with armed militia.

» Perhaps Trump cut a deal many years ago to serve the ruling elite cabal since they, too, are fighting from within, thus using Trump as needed and protecting him as such; or

» Perhaps it's miraculous and the will of God.

We can guess all day but, instead, we should:

» Become more familiar with disruptive, uncomfortable truths.

» Become a truth seeker, then a truth revealer.

» Become more active.

» Protect and preserve our health, family, and wealth.

» Pray.

Donald J. Trump was not supposed to happen. His bold and brash arrival on the scene back in June 2015 seeking the office of the presidency was not on the battle plan of the tightly controlled global agenda. Many of the issues and proposed solutions Trump has raised – such as calling out the biased media, exposing the PACS, immigration, and building the wall, the Iran deal, the U.N., the Syrian refugee influx, global trade, and ISIS to name but a few – go very much against the grain of the new global order and against the United Nations' Agenda 2030.[2] He has attacked and questioned the Iran deal and says it is so bad for America that he considers it "suspect." He has also indicated that Hillary Clinton has committed crimes and was not qualified to run for office, is being protected and perhaps belongs in jail. You see, so much progress has been made toward the new world order in the past twenty-odd years that a Donald Trump on the scene is a threat, an unwanted distraction. And so the globalists will do whatever it takes to stop the forward progress of Donald J. Trump as President. The "plants", such as BLM and others that were bussed in who were at his rallies, and the biased media, are just the tip of the iceberg.

All Attempts Have Failed

Everything imaginable has been thrown in Trump's way this far to prevent his GOP nomination, his election, his inauguration, and now his agenda from being carried out. The orchestrated attacks by the controlling shadow government have used and deployed the following in their attempts to derail and destroy Trump:

» Media
» BLM and related riots
» Multiple assassination attempts
» Threats to his children
» Skimming
» Voter fraud

2 https://johnmichaelchambers.com/global-service-announcement-agenda-2030-part-vi-2/

- » Election theft
- » The vote recount
- » Swaying the electoral college
- » The Russian false flag hoax
- » The inauguration disruptions
- » Hollywood celebrity boycotts

And the following was reported by Paul Craig Roberts on December 22, 2016:

> **"Trump himself seems to think he is in danger.** *According to MSNBC, Trump intends to supplement his Secret Service protection with private security. As there is evidence of CIA complicity in the assassination of President John F. Kennedy (film shows Secret Service agents ordered away from JFK's limo immediately prior to his assassination), Trump, who is clearly seen as a threat by the military/security complex, is not being paranoid.* **MSNBC implies that Trump's private security is to suppress protesters, as if government security forces have shown any compunction about suppressing protesters.** *"*

We will never forget what happened to JFK. God forbid this should ever happen to President Trump. God help us. God protect us. Prayers are in order to protect President Donald Trump and his family.

SECTION V: A BETTER WORLD FOR POSTERITY
Tools and Resources to Survive and Thrive

CHAPTER TWENTY-TWO: MARGARITAS AT THE POOL

I WOULD LIKE TO ADDRESS THE SUBJECT of protecting and preserving wealth as a follow-up to the inevitable market crash that is looming. In earlier chapters, as we connected the dots on the true state of the economy, the markets, and the currency itself, we can clearly see that all is not well, and the likelihood of a substantial correction of sorts is in order. So again, what to do? The answer is to hope and pray for the best, but plan for the worst.

One of many of Einstein's famous quotes is most applicable here, and that being the definition of insanity as doing the same thing over and over again and expecting different results. Simply stated? Stop. When? Now. You don't want to become part of the "Ifidda Club" now, do you? You know about the Ifidda Club, right? "Ifidda (if I had) only heeded the call and planned in advance!" Well, don't be part of the Ifidda Club. You want to know how to predict the future? By planning for it. Let's take a new approach to an old problem, shall we?

Margaritas at the Pool

I lived in Florida for about ten years. We know about hurricanes. With hurricanes there are always advanced indicators that a storm is coming. We can forecast approximately where, when, and what the severity may be. Well, there are basically two decisions to make. One is to do nothing – not highly recommended, I might add. The other is to plan for the worst.

It's really no different at all with this coming economic hurricane. You read the reports. You follow the patterns, and you can clearly see that a category five hurricane with winds up to two hundred miles per hour is coming your way. This particular storm may also bring a tremendous storm surge along with anticipated tornadoes. Now I ask you, would you be sitting by the pool with a margarita anticipating the arrival of this category five hurricane? Of course not. You would not be going about your life business as usual under these circumstances because it clearly is not business as usual being in the path of a devastating storm. So what would you be doing? Preparing for the worst in order to protect and preserve not only your home and possessions, but your life and the lives of your loved ones.

You may batten down the hatches. Tape the windows to prevent shattering glass. Raise all valuables up off the floor in the event of water damage. You might get a large supply of lumber and board up the windows and doors. You would get to the store before supplies ran out and stockpile water, not only for drinking, but for bathing. You might fill the bathtub. Sure it would be wise to have batteries, a radio, flashlights, candles, and lighters.

And since you could be without power for days or weeks and since it may be difficult to get around the neighborhood and the stores may be empty anyway (never mind price gouging), you will stock up on food, non-perishables. Maybe fill coolers with ice, medicines, etc. The list goes on and on. A prepared person would have a detailed checklist handy and simply swing into action. Some may board up and get out of Dodge altogether! The point is you would plan. Why? To minimize the damage so that you can get on with your life, business as usual, once the storm passes. Makes sense, doesn't it?

You see, what may be coming our way is a category five *economic hurricane,* but this is the hurricane of hurricanes, unlike anything we have seen before. The U.S. is in the eye of the storm, with clouds and winds surrounding us north, south, east, and west. You can't ignore this. You can't prevent it. You can't wish it away. You can't sip your margarita at the pool without expecting serious consequences. The wrong thing to do is nothing.

So, where do we begin? First by being properly informed, but the mainstream media, the government, and vested interested financial advisors and brokers have proven to be biased, unreliable sources. In fact, they tell you all is fine while, in fact, all is not fine. You must do your homework, your due diligence. You must find credible, reliable, proven sources. You must surround yourself with like-minded people who do truly understand the times in which we live. People who have expertise in the area you need help in. You need to learn how to effectively GOOTS (get out of the system). Then you must act. Not when the economic storm is two days away, but well in advance. And with the *economic storm,* you are never given advance warning, never; therefore, you must read the writing on the wall, and hopefully segments of this book have prompted you to do so, because the time for action is now, not tomorrow. You cannot prevent the storm, but you can prevent the damage. This raises an important question.

Why People Don't Act

If you have not read the "Open Letter from Me to You" in the beginning pages of this book, this is a good time to do so. Having worked with so many people when I was a financial advisor and then as a consultant for over fifteen years, I feel as though I have discovered the common denominator as to *why* people do not act when they know that something is wrong. It's procrastination. But why do people procrastinate?

Procrastination

People procrastinate because they are in doubt. This leads to fear, which leads to inaction, the deer in the headlights. They simply do not understand all the factual information. When we are in doubt about such things, it is easy to become fearful, and this leads to inaction due to a lack of confidence. Inaction (or wrong action) is based upon doubt, so there is a remedy to remove the doubt and to rise up the scale towards certainty and confidence.

Once you take a new and fresh approach to a longstanding operating basis and/or existing problem, you are on the road to unlocking inaction, moving out of fixed conditions, making sound decisions that you are confident in – and you will sleep better at night. The remedy in part consists of having the following:

» Independent, non-biased resources.
» People with expertise in the area you need help in.
» A thorough, all-encompassing, integrated plan or road map.
» GOOTS (get out of the system).
» A team of like-minded people who understand the times – similar ideology.

This subject of wealth preservation and understanding both the dangers and opportunities regarding the turbulent financial times that lie ahead is most important; however, this subject matter goes beyond the scope of this work, so I have provided additional resources and information at the back section of the book.

Chapter Twenty-Three: Discovery and the Evolution of Change

Breaking Free from the Matrix

WE ARE INDEED LIVING IN THE AGE of an increasing number of smarter phones and an increasing number of dumbed-down people. Isaac Asimov once said, "The saddest aspect of life right now is that science gathers knowledge faster than society gathers wisdom." By and large, his quote is true today.

Technology has advanced and continues to advance rapidly. We have the technology to solve many of the critical issues facing mankind and the planet today, from air to water to food, and not just for some, but for all. For each and every one of us. You know we can put an end to starvation, so why haven't we? Children are starving to death every day, and all we do is change the channel or surf another website.

The trouble, as outlined in this book, is the shadow government's systems and institutions, such as central banks and the debt-based monetary and economic systems. Governments, international bankers, corporations, Hollywood, "big pharma," secret societies, religions, and others are preventing forward progress in exchange for both profit and control and are again using a world of betrayal after trust while utilizing clever deceptive techniques.

Ultimately, I am a long-term optimist but a short-term realist. I believe that love conquers all and the light will shine, expose the evil, and overcome the darkness. This is now under way. However, I also feel we are living in a time where being a flippant, eternal optimist or a doom-and-gloom pessimist is not the most effective position to take. In fact, I believe that being a flippant optimist in the face of the harsh realities of the day can get you, and perhaps others around you, killed. In times like these there is nothing *smart* or *cool* about being a short-term optimist; don't buy it; neither is denial or burying our heads in the sand. We might consider starting out by being a realist.

Observe the obvious, trust but verify, practice critical thinking, question authority, question everything, and think for yourself. Surround yourself with people of like mind who do indeed truly understand the times in which we live, and expand those circles of relationships.

Being a realist can be challenging. One must first be able to recognize truth from something other than truth. This can be difficult, as we are living in a bubble, a falsely created reality, a contrived and controlled world strewn with lie after lie, concealed truths, half-truths, and biased vested interest for selfish gain and to assert control over the free will of others.

I mean, after all, these merchants of chaos take our space and make it small; they stamp out free will and keep us tied and bound. They direct our attention and control our minds for their evil deeds. Well, a new day has come and so this shall perish from the earth. You are not alone. We are never alone.

And so once again, the blissfully ignorant go along as though it were business as usual. It's not business as usual, and I can assure you of this. I believe we are living in extraordinary and challenging times. My mission is to awaken, inspire, and motivate people; however, only individuals themselves can become awakened, inspired, and motivated while other people can be the conduit or trigger point. I am not telling anyone how to think, for who am I, or anyone for that matter, to do such a thing? I am merely asking you to look, observe, do some due diligence, question what you see before you, and think for yourself. Fair enough?

We must stop and look around to reassess ourselves, others, life, and the systems and structures that make this world go round. If you are tired of spinning around in the hamster wheel called your life, then it's time to look at who is spinning that wheel and what you can do to stop this circular insanity. We must realize that a major paradigm shift is under way, and that we have been living in a web of deceitful lies designed to entrap us and move us away from the spirit and more towards vanity and worldly possessions as we march blindly like useless idiots down the road to serfdom. The opposite of love is not hate; it is fear, so choose love. As you obtain more and more truths, then take the correct steps in implementing change, as the fear subsides.

Many of us have become a part of what I call the robotic, hypnotic flock. Ignorant followers, so to speak. Now, being a follower is a good thing, as most of us are *not* leaders, yet we rely on leadership. When being a follower, be a wise and discerning one and not an ignorant one. Be aware of who or what ideology you are following and ask yourself if this is pro-survival, with the greatest benefit to the many without hurting the one. Then proceed. The world has been void of leadership. This has now changed as witnessed by BREXIT, bold moves made by the government of Iceland against its corrupt bankers, Putin's stance on ISIS, and GMOs for example, and most notably, and of course, with the election of Donald J. Trump as President of the United States. A new day is dawning. The human race and the universe itself are becoming more and more conscious of themselves. This is a good thing as we are a culture and civilization in serious decline, a planet in peril. A full course correction has just begun, and soon the masses will see this. In this, there is hope. You can't change people. They change themselves by their own decisions. You can influence them and guide them. We live in an age of deception and betrayal as the standard modus operandi. This is now being exposed and so this will change.

Paradigm Shift of Consciousness

We are talking about the awareness of masses of individuals in the human race and the universe itself awakening. This is taking place and rather rapidly, but sadly against alternative destructive forces that have had a head start. And now with this mass awakening within the human spirit taking place, there is hope. My heart had been longing for leaders who stand for freedom to come forth to help bring out the best and the truth of the human spirit that we may live in love and peace together. We are now embarking upon this path.

There is a spiritual awakening taking place, and it's as though we are being helped. Very privately and soulfully, people around the world are gravitating to truth as they see the evildoers for who and what they are. We must surrender to this higher calling and continue seeking truth. We must see things as they truly are. This can be taxing and perhaps a lonely journey, feeling like a bit of an outcast to the norm as the false matrix and its minions try to pull us back into their dead and dying paradigm. But we must operate with integrity. We must stay the course, listening to that higher voice from within. This is grounding and brings a sense of peace and calm.

Love yourself. Find your voice. Become a true expression of who you really are. Shout it from the rooftops. Become comfortable and reminded of the perfection and abundance that exists for you and for others. Truth is powerful, and truth leads to freedom. You can help redirect mankind on this much-needed course correction. We all have this power, this innate ability. You can move mountains. You can influence others. Together we can save America.

Discovery and the Evolution of Change

Step One: Discovery and the Evolution of Change

Arriving at the truth. This is where one begins to question things as they are and begins to embark upon what can be an uncomfortable journey, as deceitful lies are revealed and truths come to light. This is where the change really begins, as one acquires a new operating basis as a free critical thinker and truth seeker. This is the first and most important grounding and empowering step.

Step Two: Motivation Through Inspiration

Seeing life in a new light. Once lies are revealed and truths are discovered, there is an inspiration within that is almost an auto-response mechanism. The motivation accelerates almost daily simply due to the fact the "lightbulbs keep going off." One now has

acquired the ability to instantly see the game being played as the daily events unfold on the evening news, and one can now easily begin to connect the dots. This is re-energizing and prompts one to take action, moving from effect to cause, creating the desire to improve conditions in one's life and perhaps in the world around us.

Step Three: Action and Commitment

Creating a better life and a better world. This step in the process of effect to causation in creating a better life and a better world requires action and ongoing commitment. Some aspire to improve conditions in their lives and their immediate circles, while others go beyond this with a burning desire to re-set the track that mankind is on and lending support to various groups and efforts already successfully in motion. This is how we begin to restore hope towards creating a world of peace rather than a world in pieces. The wrong thing to do is nothing. Where in this three-step process are you? Where do you need to begin or focus your attention on most? Which step or steps do you need help with?

Conclusion

The second American revolution is a battle that is fought on many fronts and will be fought for many years to come. Some battles will be won, others will be lost, and along the way there are dangers to protect oneself from, as well as opportunities to take advantage of.

The challenges we all face are enormous, but the scales are tipping. This is our time; we have a chance. The time for action is now. You are nothing more than an accomplice should you stand by idly as the culture and planet decline rapidly into very unpleasant conditions. With this book, it is my hope that we realize these *misconceptions* and begin the much-needed *course corrections,* both personally and collectively. Become a truth seeker, then a truth revealer. Spread the word.

CHAPTER TWENTY-FOUR: BY THE GRACE OF GOD

WE CAN ONCE AGAIN BE THE HOPE, promise, and a beacon of light on the shining hill for all the world. There is a lot of work to be done. It will not be fast. It will not be easy, and the desired outcome is not guaranteed. But never underestimate what one man can do. Donald Trump has awakened and inspired a nation and people all over the world. In this, there is hope and promise for a better tomorrow.

By the grace of God, we may prevail. The resurrection of America has begun. Let us not squander this miraculous opportunity. I will close out the pages of this book with an optimistic message of hope from President Donald J. Trump, our new commander-in-chief who has inspired a nation and the world as he leads America through its second revolution.

Trump's Foreign Policy Speech

"Thank you for the opportunity to speak to you, and thank you to the Center for the National Interest for honoring me with this invitation. I would like to talk today about how to develop a new foreign policy direction for our country – one that replaces

*randomness with purpose, ideology with strategy, and chaos
with peace. It is time to shake the rust off of America's foreign
policy. It's time to invite new voices and new visions into the
fold."*

Donald Trump took a bold stance going up against the globalists'
agenda, as outlined here in this foreign policy speech. Things will
begin to change with an "America First" approach to foreign policy.
Trump continued...

*"The direction I will outline today will also return us to a time-
less principle. My foreign policy will always put the interests
of the American people, and American security, above all else.
That will be the foundation of every decision that I will make,
and America First will be the major and overriding theme of
my administration but, to chart our path forward, we must first
briefly look back."*

Then candidate Donald Trump illustrated, through history, our
accomplishments as a nation.

*"We have a lot to be proud of. In the 1940s we saved the world.
The Greatest Generation beat back the Nazis and the Japanese
Imperialists. Then we saved the world again, this time from
totalitarian Communism; the Cold War lasted for decades, but
we won."*

Trump went on to talk about how policy must change with the
changing times.

*"Democrats and Republicans working together got Mr.
Gorbachev to heed the words of President Reagan when he
said: 'Tear down this wall,' and history will not forget what
we did. Unfortunately, after the Cold War, our foreign policy*

veered badly off course. We failed to develop a new vision for a new time."

In this well-written and well-delivered speech, Trump indicated that we have erred and moved our nation in the wrong direction (by design, I might add).

"In fact, as time went on, our foreign policy began to make less and less sense; logic was replaced with foolishness and arrogance, and this led to one foreign policy disaster after another. We went from mistakes in Iraq to Egypt to Libya, to President Obama's line in the sand in Syria. Each of these actions have helped to throw the region into chaos, and gave ISIS the space it needs to grow and prosper."

And so nation building and spreading democracy around the world may be coming to an end soon, at least through war and occupation. Trump spelled it out in the following paragraph, along with defining what steps he will take as President with regards to foreign policy.

"It all began with the dangerous idea that we could make Western democracies out of countries that had no experience or interest in becoming a Western democracy. We tore up what institutions they had and then were surprised at what we unleashed. Civil war, religious fanaticism; thousands of American lives, and many trillions of dollars, were lost as a result. The vacuum was created that ISIS would fill, and Iran, too, would rush in and fill the void, much to their unjust enrichment. Our foreign policy is a complete and total disaster – no vision, no purpose, no direction, and no strategy, so today, I want to identify five main weaknesses in our foreign policy."

First, our resources are overextended

In this speech, Donald Trump put forward the case that these failed policies of the past and the recent past have cost the U.S.

> *"President Obama has weakened our military by weakening our economy. He's crippled us with wasteful spending, massive debt, low growth, a huge trade deficit, and open borders. Our manufacturing trade deficit with the world is now approaching $1 trillion a year."*

We are the largest debtor nation in the world, and our popularity as a nation and as a people is declining across many places. Trump spoke with conviction.

> *"We're rebuilding other countries while weakening our own. Ending the theft of American jobs will give us the resources we need to rebuild our military and regain our financial independence and strength. I am the only person running for the presidency who understands this problem and knows how to fix it."*

Secondly, our allies are not paying their fair share

Big changes coming soon. Read this.

> *"Our allies must contribute towards the financial, political, and human costs of our tremendous security burden, but many of them are simply not doing so. They look at the United States as weak and forgiving and feel no obligation to honor their agreements with us. In NATO, for instance, only four of twenty-eight other member countries, besides America, are spending the minimum required 2% of GDP on defense."*

What Trump discusses in the next paragraph is common sense. It only makes sense for these nations to contribute. When you provide something for nothing, you end up with non-optimum results. Think the long-term abuse of welfare, for example. It's no different with nations.

"We have spent trillions of dollars over time – on planes, missiles, ships, and equipment – building up our military to provide a strong defense for Europe and Asia. The countries we are defending must pay for the cost of this defense and, if not, the U.S. must be prepared to let these countries defend themselves. The whole world will be safer if our allies do their part to support our common defense and security, and a Trump Administration will lead a free world that is properly armed and funded."

Thirdly, our friends are beginning to think they can't depend on us

Trump held nothing back and assigned responsibility to Obama.

"We've had a president who dislikes our friends and bows to our enemies. He negotiated a disastrous deal with Iran, and then we watched them ignore its terms, even before the ink was dry. Iran cannot be allowed to have a nuclear weapon and, under a Trump Administration, will never be allowed to have a nuclear weapon, all of this without even mentioning the humiliation of the United States with Iran's treatment of our ten captured sailors."

As author of the best-selling book *The Art of the Deal*, Trump launched into negotiating.

"In negotiation, you must be willing to walk. The Iran deal, like so many of our worst agreements, is the result of not being willing to leave the table. When the other side knows you're not going to walk, it becomes absolutely impossible to win at the same time; your friends need to know that you will stick by the agreements that you have with them."

Trump indicated how our military defense program had been gutted by Obama over the past eight years.

"President Obama gutted our missile defense program, then abandoned our missile defense plans with Poland and the Czech Republic. He supported the ousting of a friendly regime in Egypt that had a longstanding peace treaty with Israel, and then helped bring the Muslim Brotherhood to power in its place."

Policies in the Middle East are going to change, and just in the nick of time, I might add.

"Israel, our great friend and the one true democracy in the Middle East, has been snubbed and criticized by an administration that lacks moral clarity. Just a few days ago, Vice President Biden again criticized Israel – a force for justice and peace – for acting as an impediment to peace in the region, and President Obama has not been a friend to Israel. He has treated Iran with tender love and care and made it a great power in the Middle East, all at the expense of Israel, our other allies in the region, and, critically, the United States. We've picked fights with our oldest friends, and now they're starting to look elsewhere for help."

Fourth, our rivals no longer respect us

You can clearly see how we have lost respect in many parts of the world today and not without reason. I notice this on a personal level when I am overseas. I can think of specific examples and in multiple countries from over the past five years.

> *"In fact, they are just as confused as our allies, but an even bigger problem is that they don't take us seriously anymore. When President Obama landed in Cuba on Air Force One, no leader was there to meet or greet him – perhaps an incident without precedent in the long and prestigious history of Air Force One. Then, amazingly, the same thing happened in Saudi Arabia – it's called no respect."*

Trump bravely called a spade a spade.

> *"Do you remember when the President made a long and expensive trip to Copenhagen, Denmark, to get the Olympics for our country, and, after this unprecedented effort, it was announced that the United States came in fourth place? He should have known the result before making such an embarrassing commitment. The list of humiliations goes on and on."*

Trump is not looking to make friends or win popularity contests. In this speech he called it like he saw it, and this is what, in part, got him elected.

> *"President Obama watches helplessly as North Korea increases its aggression and expands even further with its nuclear reach, and our president has allowed China to continue its economic assault on American jobs and wealth, refusing to enforce trade rules – or apply the leverage on China necessary to rein in North Korea. He has even allowed China to steal government*

secrets with cyber-attacks and engage in industrial espionage against the United States and its companies. We've let our rivals and challengers think they can get away with anything. If President Obama's goal had been to weaken America, he could not have done a better job."

Finally, America no longer has a clear understanding of our foreign policy goals

A sad commentary below.

"Since the end of the Cold War and the breakup of the Soviet Union, we've lacked a coherent foreign policy. One day we're bombing Libya and getting rid of a dictator to foster democracy for civilians; the next day we are watching the same civilians suffer while that country falls apart."

I agree with the statement below and would also like to add that Bush is guilty as charged and responsible along with Clinton and Obama.

"We're a humanitarian nation but the legacy of the Obama-Clinton interventions will be weakness, confusion, and disarray. We have made the Middle East more unstable and chaotic than ever before; we left Christians subject to intense persecution and even genocide; our actions in Iraq, Libya, and Syria have helped unleash ISIS; and we're in a war against radical Islam. But President Obama won't even name the enemy. Hillary Clinton also refuses to say the words 'radical Islam,' even as she pushes for a massive increase in refugees."

Let's hope the new DOJ goes after Hillary Clinton.

"After Secretary Clinton's failed intervention in Libya, Islamic

terrorists in Benghazi took down our consulate and killed our ambassador and three brave Americans. Then, instead of taking charge that night, Hillary Clinton decided to go home and sleep! Incredible. Clinton blames it all on a video, an excuse that was a total lie. Our ambassador was murdered and our Secretary of State misled the nation and, by the way, she was not awake to take that call at three o'clock in the morning, and now ISIS is making millions of dollars a week selling Libyan oil."

This will change when I am President

Yes, and things are changing since Donald Trump has become President. The battle has begun.

"To all our friends and allies, I say America is going to be strong again. America is going to be a reliable friend and ally again. We're going to finally have a coherent foreign policy based upon American interests, and the shared interests of our allies. We are getting out of the nation-building business, and instead focusing on creating stability in the world. Our moments of greatest strength came when politics ended at the water's edge."

True leadership has come to America and thus the world. Donald Trump is on the verge of redirecting humanity.

"We need a new, rational American foreign policy, informed by the best minds and supported by both parties, as well as by our close allies. This is how we won the Cold War, and it's how we will win our new and future struggles."

First, we need a long-term plan to halt the spread and reach of radical Islam

President Donald Trump laid out an overview of what he intends to do once in office.

"Containing the spread of radical Islam must be a major foreign policy goal of the United States. Events may require the use of military force, but it's also a philosophical struggle, like our long struggle in the Cold War. In this we're going to be working very closely with our allies in the Muslim world, all of which are at risk from radical Islamic violence."

And finally ISIS will be dealt with. The reason it has not been effectively dealt with is due to the fact that it was created by the shadow government, and Obama followed his marching orders well.

"We should work together with any nation in the region that is threatened by the rise of radical Islam, but this has to be a two-way street – they must also be good to us and remember us and all we are doing for them. The struggle against radical Islam also takes place in our homeland; there are scores of recent migrants inside our borders charged with terrorism."

Meanwhile President Obama had the audacity to tell the American people and the world that we have not had a foreign-planned terror attack on U.S. soil since he took office.

"For every case known to the public, there are dozens more. We must stop importing extremism through senseless immigration policies. A pause for reassessment will help us to prevent the next San Bernardino or worse – all you have to do is look at the World Trade Center and September eleventh."

The following statement is most encouraging, as the horrific death and destruction of many lives and nations by ISIS will soon come to an end. God bless the innocent victims.

"And then there's ISIS. I have a simple message for them. Their days are numbered. I won't tell them where and I won't tell them how. We must, as a nation, be more unpredictable, but they're going to be gone and soon."

We have to rebuild our military and our economy

Here Donald Trump laid out the deliberate obliteration of what was once the most feared and powerful military in the world.

"The Russians and Chinese have rapidly expanded their military capability, but look what's happened to us. Our nuclear weapons arsenal, our ultimate deterrent, has been allowed to atrophy and is desperately in need of modernization and renewal."

Trump made his point clear with the following:

"Our active duty armed forces have shrunk from two million in 1991 to about 1.3 million today. The Navy has shrunk from over 500 ships to 272 ships during that time; the Air Force is about one-third smaller than 1991. Pilots are flying B-52s in combat missions today which are older than most people in this room, and what are we doing about this? President Obama has proposed a 2017 defense budget that, in real dollars, cuts nearly 25% from what we were spending in 2011."

The first obligation of the President is to protect his or her country. This is now being restored and refocused with the election of Donald Trump.

"Our military is depleted, and we're asking our generals and military leaders to worry about global warming. We will spend what we need to rebuild our military; it is the cheapest investment we can make. We will develop, build, and purchase the best equipment known to mankind. Our military dominance must be unquestioned, but we will look for savings and spend our money wisely. In this time of mounting debt, not one dollar can be wasted."

The economy (over time) will get back on track.

"We are also going to have to change our trade, immigration, and economic policies to make our economy strong again – and to put Americans first again. This will ensure that our own workers, right here in America, get the jobs and higher pay that will grow our tax revenue and increase our economic might as a nation. We need to think smarter about areas where our technological superiority gives us an edge; this includes 3-D printing, artificial intelligence, and cyberwarfare."

The vets. What a disgrace. All the evil and imbalances will soon be redirected and set right.

"A great country also takes care of its warriors. Our commitment to them is absolute. A Trump Administration will give our servicemen and women the best equipment and support in the world when they serve, and the best care in the world when they return as veterans to civilian life."

Finally, we must develop a foreign policy based on American interests

America first. It's that simple.

*"Businesses do not succeed when they lose sight of their core
interests and neither do countries. Look at what happened
in the 1990s; our embassies in Kenya and Tanzania were
attacked, and seventeen brave sailors were killed on the USS
Cole, and what did we do?*

*"It seemed we put more effort into adding China to the World
Trade Organization – which has been a disaster for the United
States – than into stopping Al Qaeda. We even had an opportunity to take out Osama Bin Laden and didn't do it, and then we
got hit at the World Trade Center and the Pentagon, the worst
attack on our country in its history."*

A much-needed course correction.

*"Our foreign policy goals must be based on America's core
national security interests, and the following will be my priorities: In the Middle East, our goals must be to defeat terrorists
and promote regional stability, not radical change. We need to
be clear-sighted about the groups that will never be anything
other than enemies, and we must only be generous to those that
prove they are our friends."*

I believe more and more nations will become allies with Trump's
America.

*"We desire to live peacefully and in friendship with Russia and
China. We have serious differences with these two nations and
must regard them with open eyes, but we are not bound to be
adversaries. We should seek common ground based on shared
interests. Russia, for instance, has also seen the horror of
Islamic terrorism."*

I, for one, have all the confidence in Trump's ability to do what is right for America. Friends today may become enemies tomorrow. Enemies today may be friends tomorrow. He will get to the bottom of this, but rest assured, it's America first.

> *"I believe an easing of tensions and improved relations with Russia, from a position of strength, is possible. Common sense says this cycle of hostility must end; some say the Russians won't be reasonable. I intend to find out. If we can't make a good deal for America, then we will quickly walk from the table."*

Everything is about to change and thank God for that.

> *"Fixing our relations with China is another important step towards a prosperous century. China respects strength, and by letting them take advantage of us economically, we have lost all of their respect. We have a massive trade deficit with China, a deficit we must find a way, quickly, to balance. A strong and smart America is an America that will find a better friend in China. We can both benefit or we can both go our separate ways."*

Longstanding treaties and organizations will now change. This transition will not be smooth, in my opinion, but must be done.

> *"After I am elected President, I will also call for a summit with our NATO allies, and a separate summit with our Asian allies. In these summits, we will not only discuss a rebalancing of financial commitments, but take a fresh look at how we can adopt new strategies for tackling our common challenges. For instance, we will discuss how we can upgrade NATO's outdated mission and structure – grown out of the Cold War – to confront our shared challenges, including migration and Islamic terrorism."*

Peace through strength.

"I will not hesitate to deploy military force when there is no alternative, but if America fights, it must fight to win. I will never send our finest into battle unless necessary, and will only do so if we have a plan for victory. Our goal is peace and prosperity, not war and destruction."

Trump assigns cause and blame where it belongs, Clinton and Obama (and again I would add Bush too).

"The best way to achieve those goals is through a disciplined, deliberate, and consistent foreign policy. With President Obama and Secretary Clinton, we've had the exact opposite: a reckless, rudderless, and aimless foreign policy – one that has blazed a path of destruction in its wake. After losing thousands of lives and spending trillions of dollars, we are in far worse shape now in the Middle East than ever before."

The insane factions of the left and many democrats at large rarely ever engage in meaningful, intelligent, and respectable discourse when it comes to matters of disagreement.

"I challenge anyone to explain the strategic foreign policy vision of Obama-Clinton. It has been a complete and total disaster. I will also be prepared to deploy America's economic resources. Financial leverage and sanctions can be very persuasive, but we need to use them selectively and with determination. Our power will be used if others do not play by the rules."

Trump's negotiation, delegation, and management now pave the way for relations and results with our global neighbors.

"Our friends and enemies must know that if I draw a line in the sand, I will enforce it; however, unlike other candidates for the

presidency, war and aggression will not be my first instinct. You cannot have a foreign policy without diplomacy. A superpower understands that caution and restraint are signs of strength."

Trump has a well-documented history of forecasting events and outcomes, as well as having stated his views and challenges facing this nation for decades.

"Although not in government service, I was totally against the war in Iraq, saying for many years that it would destabilize the Middle East. Sadly, I was correct, and the biggest beneficiary was Iran, who is systematically taking over Iraq and gaining access to their rich oil reserves – something it has wanted to do for decades. And now, to top it all off, we have ISIS."

Trump style…

"My goal is to establish a foreign policy that will endure for several generations. That is why I will also look for talented experts with new approaches and practical ideas, rather than surrounding myself with those who have perfect resumés, but very little to brag about except responsibility for a long history of failed policies and continued losses at war."

Well summarized.

"Finally, I will work with our allies to reinvigorate Western values and institutions. Instead of trying to spread 'universal values' that not everyone shares, we should understand that strengthening and promoting Western civilization and its accomplishments will do more to inspire positive reforms around the world than military interventions."

These are my goals as President

It's amazing how the media and the sheeple fail to discuss the actual policies and goals of this new President, but Trump makes his position quite clear for anyone with eyes to see and ears to listen.

> *"I will seek a foreign policy that all Americans, whatever their party, can support, and which our friends and allies will respect and welcome. The world must know that we do not go abroad in search of enemies, that we are always happy when old enemies become friends and when old friends become allies. To achieve these goals, Americans must have confidence in their country and its leadership again."*

The next paragraph is common sense and historically true, but the brainwashed? Well, they are brainwashed, what can I say?

> *"Many Americans must wonder why our politicians seem more interested in defending the borders of foreign countries than their own. Americans must know that we are putting the American people first again. On trade, on immigration, on foreign policy – the jobs, incomes, and security of the American worker will always be my first priority. No country has ever prospered that failed to put its own interests first. Both our friends and enemies put their countries above ours, and we, while being fair to them, must do the same."*

To me this line summarizes the entire Trump movement; the fact that we, the people, will no longer surrender to the false song of globalism.

> *"We will no longer surrender this country, or its people, to the false song of globalism. The nation-state remains the true foundation for happiness and harmony. I am skeptical of inter-*

national unions that tie us up and bring America down, and
will never enter America into any agreement that reduces our
ability to control our own affairs."

Big changes are now under way under Trump's vision and leadership.

"NAFTA, as an example, has been a total disaster for the U.S.
and has emptied our states of our manufacturing and our jobs.
Never again. Only the reverse will happen. We will keep our
jobs and bring in new ones; there will be consequences for
companies that leave the U.S. only to exploit it later."

The following sentences are chilling when you realize what has happened to us over the past few decades. What a relief that the tides are shifting.

"Under a Trump Administration, no American citizen will ever
again feel that their needs come second to the citizens of for-
eign countries. I will view the world through the clear lens of
American interests. I will be America's greatest defender and
most loyal champion. We will not apologize for becoming suc-
cessful again, but will instead embrace the unique heritage that
makes us who we are."

Trump nails it. With strong, compassionate, wealthy, moral America, we can help make the world a better place. This movement extends to all of humanity as Trump indicates below.

"The world is most peaceful and most prosperous when America
is strongest. America will continually play the role of peace-
maker. We will always help to save lives and, indeed, human-
ity itself but, to play that role, we must make America strong
again, we must make America respected again, and we must

make America great again. If we do that, perhaps this century can be the most peaceful and prosperous the world has ever known. Thank you."

– Donald J. Trump

Thank-You Tour

The following are powerful and positive statements from President Trump's "Thank You" tour excerpted from Donald Trump's speech in Hershey PA. on December 15, 2016.[1]

> *"The American people have shown the world that we still run our country. I will never forget you. I will never, ever stop fighting for you. I will never, ever let you down. In four years we will win again and by even more. The era of economic surrender is over; you the people will have a champion who will fight for you in the White House, because from now on it's going to be America first."*

I get chills when reading this and I encourage you to watch this speech.

> *"People say we live in a globalized world, but the relationships that people value most are local, family, city, state, and country. There is no such thing as a global anthem, a global currency, or a global flag. We salute one flag and that is the American flag. Buy American and hire American."*

---

1 Trump Thank You Rally in Pennsylvania | Full Event, https://www.youtube.com/watch?v=clcpB9hC_8s

As Trump said at the Republic National Convention, "I am your voice."

> *"This is truly an exciting time to be alive. The script is not yet written, we do not know what the page will read tomorrow, but for the first time in a long, long time, what we do know is that the pages will be authored by each and every one of you. You the American people will finally be in charge again; your voice, your desires, your hopes and aspirations will never again fall on deaf ears. The forgotten men and women of our country will not be forgotten anymore."*

A new day is dawning for America and the world.

> *"We will re-establish the rule of law. Defend the Second Amendment, protect religious liberty, and appoint justices to the United States Supreme Court who will uphold and defend the Constitution of the United States. We will heal our divisions and unify our country. We will be a unified country again. When Americans are unified there is nothing that we cannot do; no task is too great, no dream too large, no goal beyond our reach."*

It's time for us all to unite.

> *"My message tonight is for all Americans from all parties, all beliefs, and all walks of life. Whether you are African-American, Hispanic-American, Asian-American, or whatever the hell you are, remember that we are all Americans. And we are all united by one shared destiny."*

Yes, by the grace of God.

"So, I am asking everyone to join this incredible movement. I am asking you to dream big and bold and daring things for your family and for your country. I am asking you to believe in yourself again and I am asking you to believe in America. And if we do that, then all together we will make America strong again, we will make America wealthy again, we will make America safe again, and we will make America great again. God bless you!"

– Donald J. Trump

In Closing

To "Make America Great Again," in my opinion, will require the guiding, protecting hand and light of God. Empower us with wisdom, strength, and protection as we continue on this path to redirect humanity, exposing and destroying those with evil intentions. Have mercy on us and protect Donald J. Trump and his family and this once great nation. Empower us and bring us back into the light of God, which never fails. We must, each and every one of us, listen closely and we must act. The hour is at hand. Freedom...it's up to US. Let the force be with you, President Trump. Let the force be with us all.

RESOURCES

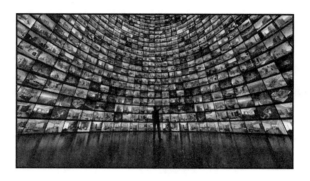

Bypass the Fake News Government Media Complex

Create an arsenal of alternative sources for information

Some Suggestions to explore below…

JohnMichaelChambers.com

President Trump

https://www.donaldjtrump.com/Promises kept

QANON –Visit links at JohnMichaelChambers.com

Get the Book "Learn About Q"

Q-The Great Awakening. What is Q. QDrops. QProofs

Plan To Save The World Remastered. We are the Plan. Dark to Light

Qanon is 100% coming from the Trump Administration

Intel – Follow on YouTube

American Intelligence Media

UniteAmericaFirst.com

Serial Brain

Robert David Steele

Kevin Shipp

X22 Report

Dr. Dave Janda

Greg Hunter

Ann Vandersteel

News Related Commentary and Reporting

http://www.amtvmedia.com/

http://www.trunews.com/

http://robertdavidsteele.com/

http://www.breitbart.com/

https://www.yourvoiceamerica.tv/author/mitchellvii/

http://thefreethoughtproject.com/

www.wnd.com

http://www.stonezone.com/

http://drudgereport.com/

https://johnmichaelchambers.com/

https://www.prisonplanet.com/

http://beforeitsnews.com/

https://www.infowars.com/

http://www.paulcraigroberts.org/

http://www.michaelsavage.wnd.com/

http://www.foxnews.com/

https://www.rt.com/

http://www.marklevinshow.com/

http://www.blacklistednews.com/

https://www.rushlimbaugh.com/

http://www.foxnews.com/on-air/hannity/index.html

http://endoftheamericandream.com/

http://www.dickmorris.com/

http://www.foxnews.com/on-air/hannity/index.html http://www.independentsentinel.com/ https://www.youtube.com/user/usawatchdog

Economy

Zerohedge.com

http://www.usdebtclock.org/

www.sovereignadvisors.net

https://www.gloomboomdoom.com/

http://trendsresearch.com/

http://www.maxkeiser.com/

http://jimrogers-investments.blogspot.com/

http://www.schiffradio.com/

https://www.lewrockwell.com/

https://www.armstrongeconomics.com/

Empowerment

http://cspoa.org/

http://tenthamendmentcenter.com/

https://realityzone.com/

https://freedomforceinternational.org/

http://www.pollmole.vote/

https://www.sovereignman.com/

https://signup.internationalliving.com/X120S104

https://www.nestmann.com/

https://www.oathkeepers.org/

http://www.shtfplan.com/

Health

www.VaccineResearchLibrary.com

www.WellnessSoldier.com

Vaxxter.com

Understanding Precious Metals

A special report by John Michael Chambers, Wealth Strategist

SECTION I: History

Before you go out and start investing in precious metals or start selling off your current holdings, it is wise to gain a better understanding about this alluring asset class so that you are better equipped to make wise decisions regarding your retirement assets. There is much to know about owning precious metals, gold, silver, platinum and palladium. No better place to start by first reviewing a brief history and by addressing some basic questions like; why gold, why silver, why now?

HISTORY

For over 6,000 years, gold has been the most sought-after form of asset protection. This is why kingdoms and governments for centuries used precious metals to back their currencies. This provided confidence in the marketplace. You have heard the expression "it's as good as gold" and you can now see how and why this statement came to be.

FLAT CURRENCY

Today we have what is called "fiat" or more accurately defined as "digital fiat currency". Fiat simply means a currency with no tangible backing (like being backed by gold and silver for example). Fiat is printed by government decree (or by the Federal Reserve as a stellar example). All currencies today are fiat currencies including the U.S. dollar. This is important to note. All fiat currencies collapse as a matter of historical reference.

SECTION II: Types of Precious Metals

GOLD: A yellow precious metal, the chemical element of atomic number 79, valued especially for use in jewelry and decoration, and to guarantee the value of currencies.

SILVER: A precious shiny grayish-white metal, the chemical element of atomic number 47.

JUNK SILVER: This is quarters, dimes and nickels no longer in circulation. They are typically scuffed up from having been in circulation. These were minted pre-1965 when they were made with 90% silver (unlike today's coins). Often purchased in large bags and can be used in a barter economy (like in Venezuela today).

PLATINUM: A precious silvery-white metal, the chemical element of atomic number 78. It was first encountered by the Spanish in South America in the 16th century and is used in jewelry, electrical contacts, laboratory equipment, and industrial catalysts.

PALLADIUM: The chemical element of atomic number 46 – a rare silvery-white metal resembling platinum.

BULLION: Both gold and silver, bars and coins of modern day issue.

SEMI NUMISMATIC: Partially rare coins, both gold and silver, minted prior to 1934 and are no longer in circulation. These coins are graded and sealed and are assigned a market value above spot price based upon condition, weight, and year. Coins like these are graded by a Numismatist. The two leading grading companies are PCGS and NCGS.

NUMISMATIC: These are exceptionally rare coins thus they are treated as a collectable and often have a very high market value. One might find these types in the Smithsonian Institute. Coins like these are graded by a Numismatist. The two leading grading companies are PCGS and NCGS.

PAPER: Precious metals are tangible assets; you can touch them. You can own them. They come in coins and bars; however, since Wall Street and the financial services industry only deal with paper assets, they have created the paper proxy version of precious metals in order to capture market share.

Some brokerage houses claim that the metals you acquire are in fact tangible. In some cases, this may be true; however, if you call and ask the brokerage to send you a bar or coin, I mean ship one to you at your address of record, you may never receive one. These are co-mingled with pooled investors and the brokerage firm stores them and uses this as leverage and margin.

You actually do not own these metals. It may be a part of your portfolio, but the metals themselves, are not yours.

Wall Street and the financial services industry only deal with paper assets; they have created the paper proxy version of precious metals in order to capture market share. They are offered in a variety of ways:

- » **I-Shares**
- » **Mutual Funds**
- » **ETF's**
- » **Stocks**

PITFALLS TO PAPER: Management fees. What if you own a mutual fund for example, and one of the mines collapses thus halting production? This affects the fund value.

When markets take serious downturns and corrections like 2008 for example, although gold and silver may be rising, your paper fund is falling. There are many reasons for this. Redemptions or liquidations. Overall market sentiment and selling frenzy will drive your paper value down, while the tangible spot prices are shooting through the ceiling. Funds, companies, currencies, banks and brokerages go out of business and sometimes the investor loses some or all of their holdings. Gold and silver have never been worth zero for over 6,000 years.

TANGIBLE METALS: These are physical tangible bars and coins both silver and gold that you actually physically own. You can take possession of them, or you can have them stored in your name at a depository.

SECTION III: Why Gold – Why Silver – Why Now?

Lack of confidence is the underlying root that sets the stage for rising prices in precious metals. However, the metals markets are also heavily controlled and manipulated (as witnessed in the past few years) due to the paper and future trading in the precious metals markets but, at some point, this will change and that point is on the horizon with the global financial reset coming and sheer market driven forces.

Before you go out and start investing in precious metals, or start selling off your current holdings, it is wise to gain a better understanding about this alluring asset class so that you are better equipped to make wise decisions regarding your investments. There is much to know about owning precious metals, gold, silver and platinum. No better place to start than by first reviewing a brief history and by addressing some basic questions like; why gold, why silver, why now?

» Chaos, social, political, geo-political, and economic uncertainty
» Metals act as a flight to safety in uncertain times
» Metals do well during rising interest rate cycles and inflationary times
» Inflation hedge
» Acts as an insurance policy against a declining or collapsing currency
» Supply and demand: supplies are limited, and demand is high

- » When the dollar weakens, gold generally strengthens
- » Silver is not only a financial metal like gold, but is also an industrial metal
- » Silver is undervalued
- » Metals are liquid, private and portable, and recognized anywhere in the world
- » Global financial and currency reset

It is important to note that interest rate cycles historically run in 28 year cycles. The last one was 32 years. With the election of Donald Trump and due to Trump's weak dollar policy as part of his plan to MAGA, we have just entered in 2017 into a rising interest rate cycle which is expected to continue for many years to come. This is bullish for gold. With manufacturing returning to the U.S. we can expect the demand for silver to increase, so buy gold, buy silver, buy now!

SECTION IV: Global Financial Reset

Some of us have heard this phrase "global financial reset" for many years now while others, for the first time, are beginning to hear this. Why? Because it is coming soon. So, what is meant by the global financial reset? In short, the global financial reset will replace the current system of how the U.S. and the world exchange for goods and services and not only for international trade. This also applies to us when we buy food, gas, pay our bills, and invest etc. You see the U.S. has been the world's reserve currency since the Bretton Woods Agreement of 1944. Well this is now, soon, coming to an end. The U.S. dollar will soon cease to be THE world reserve currency and will be replaced by a new system. Thank God Trump is in DC during such a time as this. Beyond the trending news stories of the day is an even bigger story, Setting the Stage for the Next Global Reserve Currency.

FEDERAL RESERVE AND FEDERAL EXPRESS

The gig is up. The for-profit banking cartel, (the Federal Reserve), has run its course. The Federal Reserve is now well exposed for who they are and for what they have done. The Federal Reserve is no more a government agency than Federal Express. One might consider the inception of the Federal Reserve to be "The Great Coupe of 1913", and indeed it was, as the U.S. Constitution states that only congress shall have the power to regulate the value and issuance of our currency.

This was given away to the for-profit bankers, via legislation signed into law by President Woodrow Wilson, who later in his memoirs, regretted this decision. If you are not familiar with what I am talking about, it is high time to get up-to-speed. The authoritative book on this subject is "The Creature from Jekyll Island", by the legendary author, film producer and researcher, G. Edward Griffin.

IMF

The IMF is to its participating members as the Federal Reserve is to the United States. The IMF provides support and SDR backing to certain members, (US, Japan, Russia, China, and the EU etc.). SDR's, or "special drawing rights" are a "privilege" (a debt to banks), and China was granted access almost two years ago, so these select nations are granted SDR's to provide funding, as well as stability and confidence, in a country and its currency. The Federal Reserve today is the largest purchaser of the U.S. treasuries which is, in essence, a debt to the Federal Reserve by the U.S. You can see how the IMF and the Federal Reserve, in some aspects, provide the same "service".

There are scores and scores of articles available and videos on YouTube and many are posted on a regular basis on a Facebook page I formed called The Economic Institute. There are many people who are following the global financial reset and you may want to look into this. People like Jim Rickards, Jim Willie and many others. Read more about President Trump's ^{weak dollar policy} and these other insightful and important posts titled Trump's Economic Capitalism and the Coming Collapse Blame It On Trump and Setting the Stage for the Next Global Reserve Currency. And FYI, don't let these links have you for one second believe that I am not a supporter of these policies. I am, 100%. Please do read on.

INDICATIONS OF THE GLOBAL RESET

Global sentiment against the U.S. Dollar is rising. This has been going on for quite some time now but is accelerating rapidly today. Pay no attention to the relatively recent surge in the U.S. Dollar as everything is about to change.

There are many pieces on the global chess board being moved. We are entering a rapidly increasing economic warfare battle with nations. In my view, the long-term deep state op, North Korea, has just been liberated from the clutches of the deep state (more on this view in another article) and is preparing to come aboard with Trump and the new plan. Global support for Trump is on the rise. There are the tariffs, currency devaluations, trade deficits and Trump's tax overhaul to create incentives to bring manufacturing back to America. There is De-regulation, thus paving the way for energy exploration and distribution and much more. This brings us to gold. Gold? Yes, gold.

There are no longer any currencies including ours that have any tangible backing. It is no wonder that China is the world's largest producer and purchaser of gold and China is hoarding it. They do not sell it, they keep it. It is sort of a battle for supremacy to be a competing world reserve currency.

With this global financial reset that is coming, watch gold as gold in essence becomes the "world reserve currency". Russia has now sold off all of its U.S. treasuries and is acquiring massive amounts of gold. President Trump discusses gold and the dollar in a Forbes magazine review. To increase demand for a stable currency and to prevent governments from printing willy-nilly via fiat currency, versus keeping currencies in check by a solid backing like gold, the battle rages on for currency supremacy. Who is the power being shifted and eventually taken away from? The Rothschild Central Banks, the IMF and the Federal Reserve, but not without a battle. Thus, a world in chaos.

SUMMARY

The stage is being set for a global financial reset of sorts. Exactly how and when this plays out is anybody's best guess. Could the dollar be backed by gold and a basket of commodities and the battle for the world reserve currency continues? USA and perhaps China as two competing world reserve currencies of choice? Or will we move to a one world currency? Will these events happen in stages? My guess is, it's already being orchestrated behind the scenes (actually has been for about ten years). I would say this reset will occur perhaps in 2020 sometime after the re-election of Donald Trump, but the first election of Donald Trump has thrown a wrench in the spinning spokes of the globalist's wheel and thus expect turmoil and economic warfare for some time to come. But the old order, the Rothschild Central Bank-Federal Reserve etc., system, which has seized control over money itself, has for the first time, a real formidable and present danger of being dethroned. Hooray at last!

We know what happened to Lincoln with the Confederate money and the greenback. We know what happened to JFK with E.O. 11110, and we know that Regan took a bullet to redirect him back on track to the bankster's money madness, so thank goodness President Trump has the key military protections and support, as well as his own private security detail. And thank God as he provides wisdom, courage, strength and protection for this president. But make no mistake, the global financial reset is "knock – knock – knockin' on global's door". And soon, the word will change. And the global support that we will need will happen. It is happening. And as the hearings, probes, grand juries, indictments, trials and tribunals surface and escalate for all the world to see, we shall continue to see that the rats are on the run and so buckle down as they are going to escalate the madness against us and the president creating distractions, death, division and chaos. But in the end, they lose. The great awakening is taking place. We are now winning. Trump + Time = Winning.

The global financial reset is coming. What to do? Let your voice be heard at the ballot box. Get politically active in one way or another. Buy some gold and be on the right side of history, and pray for the safety of this president and this nation.

SECTION V: Designing the Optimum Metals Portfolio

Both gold and silver are financial metals with silver also being an industrial metal. It is important to hold both gold and silver as the leading and preferred tangible metals mix.

Today, silver is trading 78 to1. It takes approximately 78 ounces of silver to buy one ounce of gold. The historical ratio average has been 20 to 1, meaning it takes 20 ounces of silver to buy one ounce of gold. This tells us that silver is undervalued and, at some point, the percentage spread gap will come back to its historical levels. So, at this time, it is wise to over-allocate into silver. We recommend 70% silver and 30% gold, but the devil is in the detail as silver can be heavy and bulky to store, so storage becomes a part of the discussion. More on storage later in another section.

RATIO TRADING: Another very important reason to over-allocate into silver now is to take advantage of the "ratio trade". As the price point differential between gold and silver narrows to that historical average, those who have over-allocated into silver can take advantage of the ratio trade simply by converting a large percentage of your silver holdings and acquire more gold. This is how one can double their gold holdings without investing one new dollar to the metals portfolio. This ratio trade opportunity has come about three times in the past 17 years and the conditions for another ratio trade opportunity are coming a bit down the pike. With this strategy, you significantly increase the dollar equivalent values of your metals holdings without investing one new dollar.

PLATINUM AND PALLADIUM: There is also a ratio between platinum and palladium. The two metals are interchangeable when used industrially, so it makes sense to watch the ratio between the two in order to see which one is undervalued. These are strictly industrial metals and, if allocated into a portfolio, should only be a small amount of the total investment allocation.

SECTION VI: Metals in IRAs (Traditional, Roth, SEP)

RETIREMENT PLANS: If you are separated from service from your previous employer or retired altogether, you should consider rolling your old plan into a self-directed IRA. Below is a list of reasons to do so. If you are still actively employed, there may be available options for you to roll over a portion of your account to an IRA. Reasons to convert.

» No longer employed-no longer contributing. Company no longer matching

» High administrative fees
» Limited investment options
» Cannot invest in physical metals
» Limited tax-advantaged distribution options at death

The IRA is a most important classification of assets. If you are not keeping place with the *real* rate of inflation (presently 6.12% and going higher), you will erode your IRA assets due to inflation, taxes, increasing required percentage of distributions and, if invested in the wrong asset classes, you also lose value due to market corrections. Consider some of your IRA in precious metals. With IRAs, you get to defer taxes on interest earned. You cannot take withdrawals if you are under the age of 59½ (exception is the 72T rule). Once you attain the age of 70½, you are required to take an increasing distribution each year thereafter. Missing a distribution results in a 50% penalty by the IRS.

IRS RULES: All IRS rules apply in a precious metals portfolio as in any asset class – the 59½ rule and the 70½ rule. You can only own bullion, bars and coins, gold and silver, inside the IRA. Semi-numismatics are not permitted.

STORAGE OPTIONS: Outside of the IRA you can take physical possession or store your metals at the depository. Inside the IRA, the metals must be stored at the depository as the IRS must know where the account inventory is stored due to custodian annual reportability rules as in any other IRA. The depository charges about $180.00 annually, regardless of how many metals you are storing.

Outside of the IRA, the depository charges ½% of the total value of the account annually. The depository is a highly secure private depository in Delaware where individuals and governments store their metals. It carries $1 Billion Dollars of liability insurance from Lloyds of London.

UNIQUE FEATURE: Some people in retirement do not rely on the IRA for income, but are forced to take their taxable distributions. Unique only to precious metals, you can take your distributions in dollars or in actual physical metals. This is very good for those who do not rely on the IRA for income as they can build a portfolio of metals at home by taking an in-kind distribution. It is still taxable but you can receive the metals instead of the dollars if you chose.

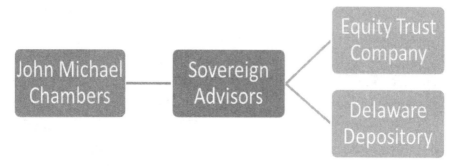

ECONOMIC INSTITUTE | An asset preservation and income planning firm offering an on-line membership and personal one-on-one wealth coach and consulting services. John Michael Chambers serves as your Strategic Wealth Coach.

SOVEREIGN ADVISORS | Resource Network referral firm from The Economic Institute. SA offers paper and tangible opportunities via private placement and precious metals, along with expert advice from a PhD Economist, Dr. Kirk Elliott.

EQUITY TRUST | ET is the third-party custodian providing year end summary statements to the account holder as required by the IRS for reportability purposes.

DEPOSITORY | Metals are purchased from and stored at the Delaware depository. The fee from this depository is about $200.00 annually and can be deducted from your metals account or paid by check.

SECTION VII: Cost of Acquisition

BUYER BEWARE

Precious metals is an unregulated industry. Not all dealers are created equally. The dealers who advertise extensively pay millions of dollars a month to reach you. The only problem is to offset their advertising costs. They simply, often at times, overcharge the customer.

Most will also charge a fee, not only when you buy it, but also when you sell it. We have done the due diligence for you so that you have the best overall value firm to acquire your metals' positions. Here's how it works:

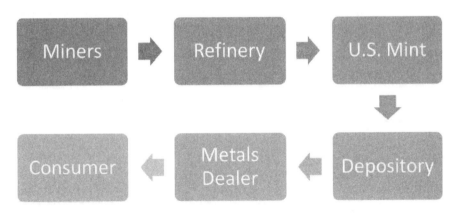

MINERS | Metals are mined typically in mountains.

REFINERY | The facility that fulfills the process which removes impurities and mints rounds or bars to a 99% purity level.

U.S. MINT | Government minted coins and bars to 99.99+% purity.

DEPOSITORY | Purchase inventory from refinery and/or U.S. mint and from the general marketplace for circulated metals.

METALS DEALERS | Purchases metals from the depository for sale to the consumer. Sells metals back to depository, or makes a secondary market to the consuming public.

CONSUMER | This is where you come in and purchase the metals from the metals dealer.

TRANSACTION COST

Metals are sold via commission. Most metals firms will charge you twice – once when you buy it and then again when you sell it. In most cases, this is not the most economically beneficial way to transact. Why? Because if you are charged on the back end too, then you will be paying a commission on the value of your account liquidation. Since most of us are buying and holding, the metals will have appreciated. Why would you want to pay a commission on the way out? If you invested $100,000 coming in and it's worth $200,000 going out, and you pay commission again on the way out, you have paid far too much.

The true competitive industry average is 8% for bullion coins and bars, gold and silver. Some firms will charge you 4% or more upfront and 4% or more back end when you sell it. It is best to pay one time only. Pay it up front.

METALS COMPARED TO REAL ESTATE

Investing is tangible metals is just that: tangible. If you buy a home (tangible), you are paying about 6% upfront to the realtor when you buy it and 6% to the realtor when you sell it. That is 12% vs. metals at 8%.

And like metals, you are typically holding your real estate for some years and selling when it has appreciated so, in essence, you are actually paying quite a bit more in real terms than 6% on the back end for real estate. It is the same for metals as you are in essence paying far more than 4% due to the appreciated value of the asset.

METALS COMPARED TO MUTUAL FUNDS

Mutual funds are very expensive. It's just that no-one reads the prospectus. The average mutual fund cost is about 3.25% annually. Even the "no load" funds are costly and they typically have back end charges should you liquidate before 5 years. With metals at 8% one-time up front and zero on the back end, you can clearly see how owning a mutual fund for a few years is far more costly than acquiring tangible metals. Also, by acquiring metals in the bull market phase, you are buying into a positive trending asset class, and although volatile, it does not take very long to make up that 8% acquisition cost. Remember, you are purchasing metals as an overall insurance policy to offset inflation and a declining currency.

DECEPTIONS AND PITFALLS

DEALERS

» Avoid national dealers who advertise on television and radio. That is a very expensive way to advertise, and the end consumer ends up paying for it.

» Avoid dealers who offer a super low price in exchange for them "storing metals for you". Many times they re-sell the same metals over and over again, knowing that not everyone will request physical delivery at the same time (similar to fractional reserve banking).

» If it is too good to be true, it probably is. For example, "We have a 1% commission". Generally, this statement is not true. They may sell at 1% more than an arbitrary internal price that is a price higher than the purchase price from the depository.

» When can that statement be true? When the dealer is a large national firm that takes a large commission on a liquidation from a client (i.e. 4%). When they keep rolling through their own inventory, they can offer a lower price up front because they made it on the liquidation. **There is a huge caution here**: at some point you will need to liquidate and you will be the person that is taken advantage of for someone else's gain.

» Depending on the state, if a dealer has a retail store front, they should collect sales tax. The tax amount would be added on to the normal commission spread of the metals being purchased.

» If they take credit cards, the dealer has to make up for the 3+% of the cost of using credit cards.

» Dealers who take cash for metals may open up their sales to federal audit as they could be complicit in money launder-ing. **AVOID** companies that take cash payments for metal purchases.

» **AVOID** coin dealers that imply semi-rare coins are not reportable. **DEALER NON-REPORTABILITY is NOT THE SAME AS TAX REPORTABLE.** Every gain or loss needs to be reported to the IRS. Deception is never okay.

SUPPORTING DOCUMENTS:

http://about.ag/goldsilverfraud.htm

https://www.aarp.org/money/scams-fraud/info-2016/gold-coin-investment-scams.html

https://www.trustedpeer.com/t/anti-money-laundering-dealers-precious-metals-stones-or-jewels/overview

https://www.law.cornell.edu/cfr/text/31/1027.210

https://www.miamiherald.com/news/local/article195552089.html

http://www.silvermonthly.com/secret-tactics-of-bullion-dealers/

COIN SHOPS

» Local coin shops do not deal in volume; therefore, retail spreads tend to be larger.

» Coin shops will not manage your account like a client. You are simply a transaction, so ratio trading strategies are not really a viable strategy unless you, the client, watch the markets on a daily basis and do it yourself.

» Depending on the state, sales tax will need to be collected.

» Hard to verify authenticity of metals purchased from local coin shops. It's better to purchase from a firm that buys directly from a U.S. depository where authenticity is guaranteed.

» **AVOID** coin shops that accept cash for metals purchases.

SUPPORTING DOCUMENTS

https://www.thermofisher.com/blog/metals/minnesota-takes-the-lead-on-regulating-the-bullion-coin-market/

SECTION VIII: The Trend is Your Friend

As mentioned earlier in this report, metals and commodities in general do very well during times of inflationary pressures and rising interest rates. One of the key rules of thumb in investing is understanding public policy, actions by the Federal Reserve, and what the impact is on various asset classes. Just remember this: "The trend is your friend". Economists the world over agree for reasons outlined in this report, that metals will outperform most other investments in the years to come. Take a look at this analysis done by PhD Economist, Dr. Kirk Elliott.

YEAR	ASSET CLASS											INFLATION MEASUREMENTS		
	30 yr	CD	GOLD		SILVER		DJIA		REAL ESTATE		CPI	ETH (TRUE INFLATION)	Upper Range
2000	6.63%	5.01%	$ 289	1.00%	$ 5.10	-0.58%	11,239.98	20.17%	$ 165,300	5.02%	3.40%	9.70%	12.13%
2001	5.54%	5.33%	$ 268	-7.18%	$ 4.52	-11.37%	10,659.26	-5.17%	$ 169,800	2.72%	2.80%	7.99%	9.99%
2002	5.45%	2.14%	$ 278	3.77%	$ 4.72	4.42%	9,876.68	-7.34%	$ 188,700	11.13%	1.60%	4.57%	5.71%
2003		1.47%	$ 347	24.94%	$ 4.84	2.54%	8,389.13	-15.06%	$ 186,000	-1.43%	2.30%	6.56%	8.20%
2004		1.15%	$ 422	21.66%	$ 6.22	28.51%	10,528.94	25.51%	$ 212,700	14.35%	2.70%	7.70%	9.63%
2005		2.08%	$ 436	3.13%	$ 6.47	4.02%	10,539.66	0.10%	$ 232,500	9.31%	3.40%	9.70%	12.13%
2006		3.28%	$ 513	17.77%	$ 8.95	38.33%	10,857.48	3.02%	$ 247,700	6.54%	3.20%	9.13%	11.41%
2007	4.85%	3.78%	$ 632	23.20%	$ 12.88	43.91%	12,565.33	15.73%	$ 257,400	3.92%	2.80%	7.99%	9.99%
2008	4.33%	3.51%	$ 833	31.80%	$ 14.80	14.91%	12,413.99	-1.20%	$ 233,900	-9.13%	3.80%	10.84%	13.55%
2009	3.13%	1.75%	$ 870	4.41%	$ 10.97	-25.88%	8,239.70	-33.63%	$ 208,400	-10.90%	-0.40%	-1.14%	-1.43%
2010	-4.60%	0.81%	$ 1,088	25.04%	$ 18.64	69.92%	10,296.09	24.96%	$ 222,900	6.96%	1.60%	4.57%	5.71%
2011	4.52%	0.48%	$ 1,406	29.24%	$ 28.31	51.88%	12,241.21	18.89%	$ 226,900	1.79%	3.20%	9.13%	11.41%
2012	3.03%	0.34%	$ 1,598	13.70%	$ 33.72	19.11%	12,605.03	2.97%	$ 238,400	5.07%	2.10%	5.99%	7.49%
2013	3.06%	0.28%	$ 1,658	3.72%	$ 31.11	-2.74%	13,760.98	9.17%	$ 258,400	8.39%	1.50%	4.28%	5.35%
2014	3.77%	0.23%	$ 1,205	-27.33%	$ 20.39	-34.46%	16,118.39	17.13%	$ 275,200	6.50%	1.60%	4.57%	5.71%
2015	2.46%	0.27%	$ 1,206	0.12%	$ 16.54	-18.88%	17,521.62	8.71%	$ 296,500	7.74%	0.10%	0.29%	0.36%
2016	2.96%	0.27%	$ 1,060	-12.11%	$ 13.86	-16.20%	16,219.86	-7.43%	$ 312,800	5.50%	1.30%	3.71%	4.64%
2017	3.02%	0.36%	$ 1,229	15.94%	$ 16.22	17.03%	22,000.00	35.64%	$ 313,100	0.10%	1.60%	4.57%	5.71%
Sum	57.27%	32.58%		172.82%		179.46%		112.16%		73.57%	38.60%	110.34%	137.67%
Annual Average	4.09%	1.81%		9.60%		9.97%		6.23%		4.09%	2.14%	6.12%	7.65%
Inflation Adjusted Return	-2.03%	-4.31%		3.48%		3.85%		0.11%		-2.03%			

RESEARCH SUMMARY			
	% OF TIME RETURN > INFLATION	ANN/AVG	ANNUALIZED AFTER INFLATION
BONDS	29%	4.09%	-2%
GOLD	59%	9.60%	3.48%
SILVER	44%	9.97%	3.85%
STOCKS	47%	6.23%	0.11%
CD	6%	1.81%	-4.31%
REAL ESTATE	44%	4.09%	-2.03%

HOW MUCH SHOULD I INVEST?

Each case varies based on many criteria. As a general rule of thumb, we believe 20% of investable assets may be, at this time, wise. The bond market is not the place to be now and for some years to come as the rising interest rate trend we are in has a negative impact on the yields in bonds and, over time, will provide a surge in metals. The stock market is at an all-time high and again echoed by most analysts and economists the world over, will come crashing down soon. Inflation is here and will continue to rise and central banks around the world continue to print currency without discretion. The global financial reset is knocking on our door. By adapting the dollar for dollar paper to tangible ratio, you are offsetting the dangers defined by acquiring the metals. Some invest more, some less. The key thing is to begin to acquire some now at this phase of the bull market.

THREE PHASES OF A BULL MARKET

PHASE ONE | Early adapters and contrarians. These individuals are getting in at the lowest acquisition cost. This is a very volatile phase of the bull market with huge moves both up and down.

PHASE TWO | The masses begin to catch on. This phase is volatile but less than phase one. We can expect two steps forward, and one step back, repeated over and over. This is typically the longest phase of the bull market. Today, in 2019, we can expect about 3-8 more years in this phase depending on many factors.

PHASE THREE | This is known as the speculative blow-off. You can see this prevalent in recent years of real estate, bubbles, tech bubbles and bitcoin bubbles. This will be no different when it comes to metals. This phase can have upward swings of 400%-600% or substantially more. Everyone is getting in. You should be getting out. This phase can go on for 6 months to a year.

SUMMARY

As of mid-2019, we are into phase two of the bull market, so come aboard now!

Dr. Elliott's Strategic Investing Course

Module 1: OPTIMIZING YOUR INVESTMENTS FOR SAFETY AND GROWTH
https://www.youtube.com/watch?v=y1DU7BYPFxI&feature=youtu.be

- Identifying market cycles.
- The government "fix".

- True state of the global economy.

- Identifying opportunities in Stock, Bond, Real Estate and Precious Metals Markets.

Module 2: HOW TO BEAT INFLATION

https://www.youtube.com/watch?v=zoUThtx-jrI&feature=youtu.be

- How inflation begins.

- Implications of inflation.

- Policy response to inflation.

- How to make inflation work for you and not against you.

Module 3: OWNING GOLD

https://www.youtube.com/watch?v=LTl9oG3F3uQ&feature=youtu.be

- History of currency.

- Types of gold for physical delivery.

- Pros and cons of gold ownership.

- Costs of ownership.

Module 4: OWNING SILVER

https://www.youtube.com/watch?v=C9UOu5vkTpc&feature=youtu.be

- Conditions that cause silver to move in price.

- Types of silver for physical delivery.

- Pros and cons of silver ownership.

- Costs of ownership.

Module 5: PROTECTING YOUR IRAS WITH PHYSICAL PRECIOUS METALS

https://www.youtube.com/watch?v=bi0YouPHVcQ&feature=youtu.be

- Inflation is not what you think.
- Inflation adjusted returns on stocks, bonds, CDs, real estate and precious metals.
- How to own precious metals in an IRA.
- Pros and cons of owning precious metals in an IRA.
- Storage and distribution of precious metals in an IRA.

HOW NATIONS DIE

https://www.youtube.com/watch?feature=youtube&v=LtyKOGTiGh Q&app=desktop

- Comparative analysis of the Roman Empire with modern day United States.
- Analysis of how a country transitions into a welfare state.
- Success strategies for thriving in these conditions.

ASSET CLASS COMPARATIVE ANALYSIS

https://www.youtube.com/watch?v=pBoJIh2NJXc&feature=youtu.be Robust yearly analysis of Stocks, Bonds, CDs, Real Estate, Gold, Silver from 2000-2017.

- Analysis of the safest investment categories moving forward.

GOOTS
Get Out Of The System

GOOTS – Yes get out of the system. But how? Keep reading...

Again, while so many others will continue to operate in the deceitful and flawed modalities being advised by an industry they no longer trust, you need not be a part of this flock. A great change has just begun. The time or action is now. Remember, Wall Street does not have main street's best interest in mind, and neither does the Federal Reserve and the globalists. The President is addressing this. It is up to you to protect and preserve your hard earned assets to survive and thrive through its paradigm shift of economic and monetary policy. Then keep fighting the good fight to help this great President resurrect America.

If you have read the entire contents of this report, along with my good friend Dr. Elliott's Strategic Investing Course, then you are more than likely have come to the conclusion that it is time to GOOTS. The following summarizes just how to do this. This is a superior sound approach to protecting and growing one's assets at this precise time in history.

Brokers never discuss it. Why? They cannot sell tangible assets. It's not part of Wall Street's Club, but this does not mean you should not own tangible assets. Specific to this model, we're talking about precious metals (tangible gold and silver) and real estate. A minimum of 20% of one's investable assets is wise at this time to be allocated into precious metals. The majority of us are allocated 100% into paper assets denominated in US dollars trapped within a fatally flawed system that is about to be overhauled. GOOTS!

Myth Of Diversification

22 Asset Classes

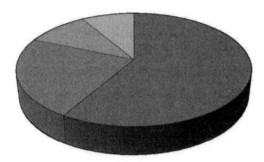

Another Wall Street mantra is "You will be just fine with diversification." Oh really? How did that work out for you in 2001? 2008? Or the month of December 2018? Not so good. You are diversified all right into a pool of paper denominated Titanics. The key is less diversification and not more. Invest in the asset classes that respond well to the current economic and monetary policies. GOOTS!

Trend Is Your Friend

Positive Trending Asset Classes

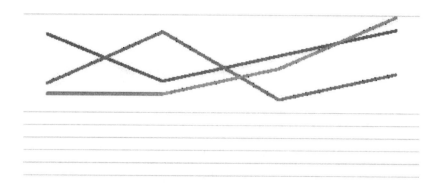

Less diversification into the right assets classes, especially under stressful changing and uncertain times is most wise. Forget the Wall Street and broker's mantra. Identifying the assets classes that respond favorably to the current policies is key. Ride the trend up and identify when cycles are shifting and don't ride the trend down.

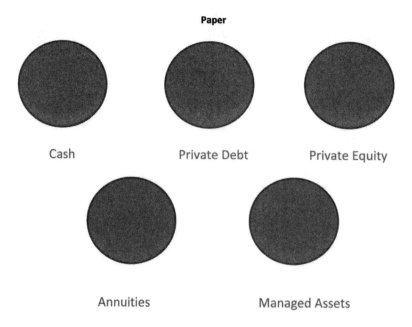

Cash: Cash is trash, but is needed for day-to-day living, as well as emergencies and opportunists. Keep some at home. This is not the time to hold an excessive amount of cash.

Private Debt: Companies not traded on the stock exchange offering attractive short-term notes with a higher than average rate of interest paying out income. No stock risk, no bond or interest rate risk.

Private Equity: Perhaps most suitable for accredited investors. Non-publicly traded companies offer opportunities to convert issued warrants into convertible shares at a greatly reduced share price.

Annuities: Not all are created equal. Suitability is key. A highly rated insurance carrier provides layers of protection and many provide guaranteed income without annuitization.

Managed Assets: For those who desire to remain fairly well invested in equities, consider hiring a private asset manager who is a fiduciary. Expect better management, no sales charges and reduced costs. Flexibility to allocate into the right sectors.

Tangible

Precious Metals

Real Estate

Precious Metals: Owning both gold and silver is most important to act as a hedge against inflation and a devaluing currency. Chaos and uncertainty are good for metals as it acts as a flight to safety. Furthermore, it responds favorably in a market correction, dollar revaluation and rising interest rates. Metals can be held inside or outside of the IRA.

Real Estate: Real estate, as you have learned from this report, will be correcting downward for some years to come. Owning real estate outright or with a low rate non-adjustable mortgage for those who are good at and like to manage real estate, and real estate for investment property with an increased pool of prospective tenants, may be wise as an income-producing asset And of course, when cycles revert and, over time, real estate, the price of real estate will resume its upward path.

The Advisor Scorecard

Do You Have the Right Team in Place?

Surveys indicate that people do not have faith, trust nor confidence in politicians, mainstream media, Wall Street and the financial services industry at large. Having the right team in place is critical and can mean the difference between a secure comfortable lifestyle and a lifetime of worry and despair.

The advisor scorecard may help you gain a better understanding of the advisor you are presently working with, and may prove to be the catalyst which paves the way to securing an independent non-biased team approach to your investments, savings and retirement assets.

Want to know how to predict the future? By planning for it! It's not business as usual in the world today, you can be assured of this. It's time for a new approach, new opportunities. Be the CEO of your life and take a new approach to managing your assets. Perhaps it's time to bring aboard additional experts to your team?

The Advisor Scorecard

1. How many years has your advisor been in the business?
2. How many years has he or she been with the firm they are presently with?
3. Which license do they have?
4. Are they in good standing with the governing regulators?
5. How are they paid? Fee based? Commissions? Both?
6. Any industry certifications or accomplishments?
7. Is your advisor a general practitioner or do they have expertise in retirement planning?
8. Is your advisor "captive" or "independent"?
9. Does his or her ideology differ from yours?
10. Can he or she offer private equity or private debt offerings?
11. What proactive suggestions have been made in light of Trump's "weak dollar policy"? Are you positioned properly?
12. Does your advisor take a "proactive" or "reactive" approach when advising?
13. Does your advisor discuss "paper to tangible" ratios?
14. Is your portfolio adequately positioned to counter rising inflation?
15. Has your age, tax bracket, growth and income needs been discussed before investing?
16. Are your beneficiary documents up-to-date?
17. Does your advisor contact you for periodic reviews?
18. Has your advisor discussed your exit strategy for any given investment?
19. Has your estate plan been discussed?

20. Has tax favored multi-generational IRA planning been discussed and established?
21. Is your advisor a creative 'outside the box thinker' or just marching to the beat of Wall Street's drum?
22. Do you know the ratings of your investments?
23. Do you know the often hidden costs of investing? Internal fees, broker fees etc.?
24. Do you have proper and adequate health and life insurance in place?
25. Is your health, life and annuity company on the "financial watch list"?
26. Has your advisor offered physical *tangible* precious metals like gold and silver?
27. We are in a rising interest rate environment which typically runs in 20+ year cycles. This just began with the election of Donald Trump as President. This will have a negative impact on bond yields. Are you still holding bonds?
28. Does your advisor understand the political and geo-political events of the day and how this may affect the economy and your portfolio?
29. Is your advisor fully aware of the gargantuan debt bubble and unfunded liabilities of the government (this includes the quadrillions in derivatives) and the looming impact that this will have?
30. Most economists the world over agree that a market collapse of magnitude is on the horizon. Are you presently insulated against this?
31. What is our advisor's plan to hedge against stock and bond risk beyond stock and bond "diversification"?
32. Has your income been secured? Are your income-producing assets subject to stock and bond risk?
33. Inflation is not 2%-3% as reported, but rather much higher

and soon on the rise. Are you keeping pace with the real rate of inflation?

34. Are you wisely and carefully invested in the positive trending asset classes or just "diversified" into many stocks and bonds?

35. Do you have adequate cash and/or liquidity for emergencies and opportunities?

36. Will you outlive your income?

37. Is the Annuity you own suitable, cost-effective and competitive?

38. Does your advisor recall the collapse of 2001 and 2008? What provisions are presently in place for the forecasted collapse that is on the horizon?

Summary

The wrong thing to do is nothing. The other wrong thing to do is the same thing over and over again expecting different results.

The advisor scorecard may help you gain a better understanding of the advisor you are presently working with, and paves the way to securing an independent non-biased team approach to your investments, savings and retirement assets. Want to know how to predict the future? By planning for it! It's not business as usual in the world today, you can be assured of this. It's time for a new approach, new opportunities. Be the CEO of your life and take a new approach to managing your assets.

The Team Approach

Wealth Strategist

John Michael Chambers is not a financial or investment advisor, nor does he manage money for a fee. John serves as a wealth strategist providing independent non-biased commentary and analysis.

John's proprietary model is truly a paradigm shift in thinking, offering his clients a new sound, superior, proactive approach to protecting and preserving wealth, utilizing both alternative paper assets, as well as tangible assets, while so many others will continue to operate in the deceitful and flawed modalities being advised by an industry they no longer trust. A great change is now upon us. The time for action is now.

As a wealth strategist, John assists like-minded individuals using his proprietary model for growth, income, proper risk assessment and asset preservation. When working with John, you gain access to John's valuable Rolodex, a resource network of like-minded financial professionals who can become part of your team.

Background

John Michael Chambers retired from a successful career from 1996-2008 as an independent financial advisor with six offices in Colorado, Florida, and New Mexico, with a focus on wealth preservation. He has been interviewed by the Wall Street Journal, as well as many other newspapers and radio and television stations of note across the country, including CBS and NBC. He retired from this successful career in 2008.

Are You Prepared for the Global Financial Reset?

Schedule a free consultation with John
E-Mail: John@JohnMichaelChambers.com

Disclaimer

John Michael Chambers is a political and economic author, speaker and publisher that does not act as a personal investment advisor for any specific individual, nor does John advocate the purchase or sale of any security or investment for any specific individual. The JMC Wealth Strategist program provides published books, reports and informative and educational modules and delivery systems, including personal one-on-one coaching and consulting and includes the John Michael Chambers Report.

Investment advice or the acquisition of precious metals, securities, insurance products and other related opportunities both paper and tangible, are not provided by John, but are offered via a referral resource network of which clients gain access to. Clients should be aware that investment markets have inherent risks and there can be no guarantee of future profits. Likewise, past performance does not assure the same future results.

John offers a free 15-minute consult to discuss your situation and to determine whether or not John's wealth strategist services are a fit for one another.

While so many others will continue to operate in the deceitful and flawed modalities being advised by an industry they no longer trust, you need not be a part of this flock. A great change has just begun. The time for action is now.

Empowering Individuals in a Changing World

John Michael Chambers Report

Geopolitical. Economic. Intel

Informed. Empowered. Connected

Surveys indicate that people no longer trust the media for news, politicians for the truth, or that Wall Street has main street's best interests in mind. The John Michael Chambers Report informs and empowers individuals in a changing world. Americans are starving for truth in this rapidly changing world. Be informed and empowered. Stay connected.

Subscription Benefits

News behind the news

An On-Line Delivery System -sent to your e-mail inbox every Sunday at 6:00 AM

News Behind the News – Weekly informative links (data, reports, and videos) carefully researched from numerous independent sources addressing current political, geopolitical, intelligence and economic content

Resources

John's featured article of the week

John's weekly video update

Important announcements, invitations and red alerts

Digital PDF copies of all published books authored by John Michael Chambers

Access to consult with John and his resource network

Subscribe to the John Michael Chamber's Report today for the low price of $7.99/mo

Be informed and empowered. Stay Connected

https://johnmichaelchambers.com/

800.986.1383

GOD BLESS THE USA